# Bill Foulkes

**United** in Triumph and Tragedy

# Bill Foulkes

**United** in Triumph and Tragedy

*The story of a Manchester United legend*

Bill Foulkes with Ivan Ponting

Published by Know the Score
Printed by Cromwell Press, Trowbridge, Wiltshire

ISBN 978 1 905449 78 1

**Mixed Sources**
Product group from well-managed
forests and other controlled sources
www.fsc.org  Cert no. TT-COC-2082
© 1996 Forest Stewardship Council

£16.7, 399/796.334092

**Acknowledgments** Bill Foulkes and Ivan Ponting would like to thank the following:
Sir Alex Ferguson, Albert Scanlon, Sir Bobby Charlton, Cliff Butler, David Meek,
David Sadler, Harry Gregg, Nobby Stiles, Roger Hunt, Tony Dunne, Andy Cowie and
all at Colorsport, Colin Wilkinson and Michael March.

All photographs courtesy of the author's collection and Colorsport with the
exception of Hulton Getty (page 11 photo section, top image) and Howard Talbot
Photography (page 22 photo section, bottom image).

# Contents

# Foreword

## by Sir Alex Ferguson

IT'S A genuine pleasure to offer a few words in tribute to Bill Foulkes. Despite all the success we've enjoyed in recent years, he remains one of the strongest characters ever to play for Manchester United and his name will be ingrained forever in its history.

Bill was one of the Busby Babes, he lived through the Munich air disaster and he was still there ten years later when United won the European Cup. So he saw the destruction of the team, with all the human tragedy that entailed, and then its resurrection and ultimate fulfilment.

Among the players, there's only Bobby Charlton who can equal that. Of course, Bobby's name is enshrined as one of the greatest world-class footballers of all time, but you can't dismiss Bill's contribution, which was massive. They did not have all the same qualities as players, but they did share commitment, determination and dedication to the cause.

When it comes to the resolve he showed in helping to rebuild the club after Munich, Bill was a product of his time. The people of that era were harder, they were brought up to be tough and self-sufficient, whereas youngsters coming into our set-up today are used to a softer lifestyle, thanks to improvements in nutrition, working and living conditions, and technology.

Bill came from a mining community and worked down a pit himself, so he embodied the steely values of that environment.

Mining folk were imbued with the loyalty factor. Neighbours used to rely on each other, always ready to help those who were going through harder times than themselves.

I believe there is a telling analogy between football and mining, and it has never been drawn more vividly than by Jock Stein. He said that when you're down in the bowels of the earth and you can't see a thing, the man next to you is your greatest friend. No matter who he is, you rely on him. It's the same with football – and Bill Foulkes' approach to his job summed that up perfectly.

Every team needs a soldier who will go through anything – and I'm gazing at a picture of Steve Bruce as I say this, which might make the point to younger readers. In all the United teams, from Sir Matt's right through to today's, you've had your famous personalities and you've had your soldiers. You don't pick 11 players who can keep the ball up a hundred times. You need a blend of contrasting types.

Going off at a tangent for a moment, the difference between the stars and the rest reminds me of a story about Bill Shankly's team talk when Liverpool were due to visit Old Trafford in the 1960s. In his typical style he was assessing the United team: 'Stepney, I don't fancy him, never did fancy him; Brennan, just a terrible player; Dunne, he's not up to much, you can get at him.' And he went on like this, assassinating everyone in the United team until he came to Best, Law and Charlton.

Now Shanks was a clever bugger, and he knew that he couldn't analyse those three in the same dismissive manner or he'd lose all credibility. So he just said to his boys: 'Well, if ye cannae beat three players, then there's something bloody wrong with ye!' Of course, there was method in his madness. He wasn't really detracting from the United lads, or meaning that they were poor players; he was just building up his own team.

In fact, while Sir Matt had his world-class trio, the likes of Bill, Shay Brennan, Tony Dunne, Paddy Crerand, Nobby Stiles and the rest could do the business week in and week out, providing a certain standard of consistent performance which mirrored their character.

Bill typified that, which is why he played nearly 700 games for United. Just like Denis Irwin, he would have been turning in eight-out-of-ten performances all the time. He wasn't the star who scored the winning goal every week – although he even managed that on one indelibly memorable evening in Madrid!

I grew up in Glasgow but I fell under the spell of Manchester United from an early age because they had a Scottish manager who had achieved huge success. The first time I saw them was in the Coronation Cup in 1953, when they beat Rangers and then lost to Celtic. I lived just down the road from Ibrox, where Spurs were playing Hibernian, but I chose to go up to Hampden to see United instead. So the romance was already there.

Then came the disaster and everyone remembers what they were doing on that day. I was in the library studying and then I went to train with my junior team. But when I got to the ground it was strangely silent. Training had been cancelled. Oh yes, the crash had a huge impact north of the border.

The Busby Babes' matches which stand out most vividly in my mind are the European Cup semi-finals against Real Madrid in 1957 when Bill was playing right-back against the famous Francisco Gento. Phew, he was a bit slow, him!

At the time Bill was not one of the better-known players, but then Munich catapulted him into the limelight. After that, as a formidable centre-half, he became a foundation stone of everything United achieved, culminating in the European Cup Final of 1968. It's truly amazing to think that Bill was 36, and carrying a serious knee injury, when he went out and mostly dominated big Jose Torres of Benfica.

There would have been two reasons why Sir Matt would have picked Bill for that final, even if his leg had been hanging off. One would have been that he knew he could depend on him in any situation, but I think the most important aspect would have been loyalty. He deserved to play. He had taken such a huge part in the rebuilding of the club. He had been there at the start of it all. Bill had a cause, a great cause, to play in that game.

Obviously, Bill was a dominant personality in that team, a very hard man, and nobody liked to play against him – some of the stories I have heard would make your hair stand on end! – yet still he strikes me as quite a shy person, a very modest fellow who has gone through a life in football at the top level, yet who has kept his feet firmly on the ground.

If asked about his great days, he would say no more than that he had done his job. I find that's a characteristic of great men. They don't have vanity; they keep their humility.

Such staunch but unspectacular servants to a club will never get the same accolades as the stars, so Bill will never be profiled like Bobby, Denis or George. But his down-to-earth qualities made him a vital part of the team, and his fellow professionals will never forget that.

Bill Foulkes deserves every shred of credit which comes his way, and he will be honoured forever at Manchester United.

**Alex Ferguson,**
Old Trafford

# One

# My privilege

LUCK, MORE than any other factor, can make or break a life. Hard work, talent, courage, integrity, dedication, loyalty ... they all play crucial parts in shaping a man's existence, and he needs all of them and more if he's going to be successful; but if Dame Fortune fails to favour him with her smile, then he hasn't got a hope. On me, she has positively beamed.

Throughout the second half of the 20th century, and into the new millennium, I have made my living at football, and I continue to be actively involved at the time of writing. For the first two decades or so, I served Manchester United, a club I have always considered to be the finest in the world, and along the way I scaled peaks which not even the most wildly optimistic of soothsayers might have predicted for a young fellow whose natural ability was decidedly limited in comparison to that of his starry colleagues.

As a Red Devil I was a member of four Championship-winning sides; I took part in three FA Cup Finals, one of which ended in victory; I played for my country; I was privileged to grow up alongside the most breathtakingly gifted set of young footballers ever to be assembled, and I was guided by the most inspirational of all managers, Sir Matt Busby. In such uplifting company I was one of the British trailblazers in continental competition, and on a balmy Wembley evening in May 1968, no less than 18 years after my arrival at Old Trafford, I played my part as United became the first English club to capture the European Cup.

But even that glorious litany of adventure and achievement does not begin to encompass the true measure of my priceless good fortune. That became vividly evident one wintry afternoon in February 1958 on a slushy airport runway, when the plane carrying us home from a European Cup quarter-final in Belgrade crashed on take-off following a refuelling stop in Munich.

I was spared – incredibly, I suffered barely a scratch – as 23 fellow passengers, including eight of my team-mates, perished as a result of the accident. Two more were maimed, never to play again, while others would bear hideous psychological scars which surely blighted their subsequent progress.

Yet just 13 days later, along with fellow survivor Harry Gregg, I was back in action for Manchester United, with so many highlights of my career still in the future. True, there were some harrowing times, too, on the path to fulfilment but, in general, fate continued to be overwhelmingly kind, as I hope I make clear in the story between these covers.

As I pondered on my experiences, a long-ago conversation with Tommy Docherty kept springing to mind, one in which he spoke of the rare privilege of lining up with a truly great player, Tom Finney, during his Preston North End heyday. Similarly, Jack Charlton had waxed lyrical to me over his experience of earning a crust alongside the majestic Welshman, John Charles, at Leeds United. Both the Doc and Jack spoke with humility of their luck – that word again – and it emphasised to me that I had been many times blessed. After all, I had been team-mate to a succession of soccer immortals – the likes of Johnny Carey, Duncan Edwards, Tommy Taylor, Bobby Charlton, Denis Law and the incomparable George Best – so if Tommy and Jack judged themselves fortunate, what did that make me?

Of course, my lifetime in soccer has been about rather more than glory and tragedy. Along the way I have encountered a cavalcade of contrasting characters, the most remarkable of whom I examine here, as well as reliving some of the quirkier events to befall me. For instance, having to con Matt into giving me my debut; going AWOL from the Army and travelling to United matches in disguise to avoid the Military Police; the double life of a coal-mining England international – you get the idea.

In the years after leaving Old Trafford, I have trotted the globe as a coach, before returning to Manchester, where I have continued to work with youngsters, trying to help them to realise their own potential in the game which I still love every bit as passionately as the first day I kicked a ball in anger.

The chronicle of my lifelong footballing journey is laid out here, honestly, simply and as accurately as memory permits. Is it the tale of a lucky man? I invite you to judge for yourself.

# Two

# Chip off the old block

FOOTBALL HAS dominated my existence for what seems like forever. In dramatic contrast to some of my fellow professionals, I've always known that the game is not quite a matter of life and death, but there has been no escaping the fact that, down the decades, it has brought in the bread and butter for the Foulkeses. As a result I have treated it with all the seriousness and commitment which I believe any family man should bestow on his means of making a living, and yet – how strange it feels to say this now – there was a time when football meant little or nothing to me.

In fact, during my formative years in the little Lancashire coal-mining village of Thatto Heath, near St Helens, soccer was never mentioned in our household, and that despite the fact that my father, Jim, had been a goalkeeper at Football League level with New Brighton. He had featured for the now-defunct Merseyside club before the Second World War when they had held their own as members of the old Third Division (Northern Section).

The truth was that we were very much of a Rugby League persuasion, hardly surprising when you consider that my grandfather, Tom Foulkes, had excelled as a full-back for St Helens and England during the early years of the 20th century, that he had captained the Saints and then gone on to become a stalwart on the club committee.

Indeed, to this day I treasure Grandad's international cap, even though I have parted with many of the medals and trophies which accumulated during my own career chasing a round ball.

To be strictly honest, my earliest sporting memories don't concern either footballing code but crown green bowls, which I watched my father and grandfather play frequently in the public parks around St Helens. Taylor Park is one I recall particularly clearly, with Grandad sitting at the entrance with his cronies, having a chat and a smoke. This would have been during and after the war when he was in his nineties but still a remarkably strong man.

There were plenty of greens and we spent a lot of time on them. I suppose I must have been reasonably apt at most games, because I picked that one up pretty quickly and became a bowler myself by the time I was ten.

It was rugby, though, which really ruled the roost at Thatto Heath and although I don't remember any major altercation in the family circle when I turned to soccer, I guess both my grandfather and father must have been a tad disappointed by my decision.

What brought it about was moving house, only a couple of miles down the road, but – and this was crucial – away from rugby-orientated Thatto Heath and into the soccer stronghold of Rainhill. Looking back, it's amazing how two neighbouring villages within the same wider community could contrast so vividly in their sporting affinity. After the move my pals played rugby at school and I played soccer, but I compromised by throwing myself into both in my spare time.

I was never an archetypal soccer-mad kid who supported one club and never missed a home match. Even after my switch of sporting allegiance I was far more likely to watch St Helens at Knowsley Road and I was about 12 when I first saw professional soccer. That day Dad took me to Anfield to see Liverpool against Charlton Athletic, and that was because he was a fan of Sam Bartram, the giant red-headed north-easterner who kept goal for the Addicks. Sam was a magnificent performer and one of the game's great characters, who always struck up a friendly rapport with the fans. It's difficult to credit that he never won a single England cap, even though the brilliant Frank Swift of Manchester City, and plenty of other fine custodians, were around at the time. As I shall discuss later, I believe that the selection committee which held sway during that period had a lot to answer for.

Certainly Dad, who was a good mate of the celebrated Liverpool 'keeper Elisha Scott and knew a thing or two about net-minding from his days between the New Brighton posts in the 1920s, was convinced that they did. Mercifully, at that point such political machinations were way above my head, and I concentrated on enjoying as much sport as possible, whatever the variety.

In my early teens I remained equally enthusiastic about rugby and soccer. As a rugby full-back I got as far as being asked for a trial by St Helens, which must have pleased my grandfather. But particularly after the move of house, I was playing also as a centre-forward or centre-half, in fact pretty well everywhere except in goal. Usually I was turning out for Prescot Celtic in a local league and before that had represented St Helens Schoolboys.

My school was Whiston Secondary Modern where a wonderful man named Mr Churchward had a huge effect on my development as a player. Nobody organised football for the local lads until he came along, but after his arrival we seemed to spend most of our time playing the game.

Sometimes, though, people get the wrong impression of my early soccer experiences. Although I hailed from a mining area, it was nothing like, say, the famous one of Ashington in Northumberland, where Bobby Charlton originated. That was a more extensive comminuty and Bobby has often mentioned the massive games, with an ever-changing cast of up to 30 per side, that would go on all day near his home, in the streets or perhaps on wasteland. Ours was a more rural environment, and most of our kickabouts were in farmers' fields.

Playing for the school team, I guess I did okay. The highlight was a measure of success in the Daily Dispatch Cup, which attracted sides from the whole of the Merseyside area. There were some big schools involved but we were giant-killers, really, just a little team from nowhere, and although we lost the final 2-1 to St Sylvester's, people began to take notice of some of our players. For my efforts I was selected for St Helens Schoolboys, and my football took off from there.

I wasn't a particularly big lad, though I was lean and pretty resilient, but one of my friends who seemed like a young giant was Derek Hennin, who went on to play for Bolton Wanderers. I faced him many a time, including at Wembley in the emotional post-Munich FA Cup Final of 1958. Even in those days he seemed like a full-grown man, big and muscular, but although he adopted a physical approach to the game, he was a fine technical player, too.

I left Whiston Secondary Modern when I was 14 at the end of the war in 1945, and I cast around for a job. The main employments in the villages were coal-mining and agriculture, while quite a few locals worked for the cable company at Prescot. Apart from in St Helens, there were plenty of positions to be found in Widnes and Warrington, and there seemed no shortage of work.

With my dad being a miner – he spent years at the coal face, then switched to a surface task, weighing the coal as it came up – and the secretary of the Miners Union for the North West area, it might have seemed inevitable that I would head for the pit, but he had always been adamant that I would not do that. He knew all too well about the risks and the hardships, and didn't want that life for me.

So for about a year I was apprenticed as a carpenter with Pilkington Glass, where I progressed satisfactorily, but still at the back of my mind – or often right at the front! – I had not given up hope of a career in professional sport. In all fairness, Pilkington were fine from that viewpoint. They worked Saturday mornings but when I wanted time off to play for Prescot Celtic, it was never any problem. I can remember asking to be excused so I could play in an important cup game at Southport, and the boss could not have been more understanding. He said I could always have time off for football.

So that was great, but there was another pressing problem, quite simply that I was not getting enough money. I can't remember exactly what I was being paid, but it was hardly anything. My father understood the need of a young fellow for a few shillings to jingle in his pocket, so he found me a job in a brass foundry only five minutes away from our home in Rainhill.

That was fine until I discovered that the noxious fumes from the foundry were bad for the chest, that in time it could severely inhibit my breathing. I decided right away that was wrong both for my general health and any sporting prospects I might harbour. I explained to the boss, who was a good friend of my father's, and he was very understanding.

After that I tried life as a painter and decorator, only to find that almost as bad for fumes. So I was moving rapidly from job to job, and for a while I despaired of finding the right one.

Meanwhile I was still doing pretty well at both footballing codes, and would have been ecstatic at the prospect of full-time employment in either. Soccer-wise I was turning out regularly for Prescot Celtic alongside Derek Hennin. One day, out of the blue as it seemed to me, Derek was asked to go for a trial with Bolton Wanderers, and they wanted me to accompany him. At first I couldn't believe it; could this be the answer to my dreams? But then I was brought rudely down to earth when Derek's dad, who ran our team, pointed out that the trial with the mighty Trotters – then a huge power in the game and holding their own in the top division – coincided with a big cup match for Prescot Celtic, and that he couldn't spare both of us at once. So Derek went to Burnden Park on his own, he impressed, and duly he was signed. I was delighted for him but was immensely upset at missing my own chance, because I knew there was no guarantee that it would ever come again.

In fact, I was angry and determined enough to leave Prescot as a result, and I joined another local team, Whiston Youth Club, which was something of a home from home to me. It was local to where I lived, I knew all the people and I fitted in immediately. They had two teams, one open-age and the other under-18. I played for both, leading the attack for the seniors and playing at centre-half for the juniors.

I suppose I must have acquitted myself reasonably because one day, after taking the defensive role in a local cup final which we lost 5-1, I was buttonholed by the Whiston president and told that I had been invited for a trial with Manchester United. It was 1949 and they were at the height of their immediate post-war glory, having won the FA Cup against Blackpool the previous year in one of the most memorable Wembley matches of all time. Apparently I had been spotted by their scout for the Liverpool area, George Davies. I could hardly believe it although, even then, there seemed an element of destiny involved, as I had been discovered in a cup final by the real cup holders.

Yet for all United's illustrious stars – the likes of Johnny Carey, Jack Rowley, Stan Pearson and Charlie Mitten – and the publicity surrounding their enterprising and inspirational young manager, Matt Busby, they meant nothing to me at the time. Oh, I had listened on the radio as they had defeated Stanley Matthews and company by four goals to two, and been impressed at the manner in which they fought back from behind, but I'd never had any particular ambition to play for them. The same could not be said for a future footballing partner of mine, a six-year-old Mancunian name of Norbert Stiles, who had become so excited as the game had approached climax that he got his head stuck between the bars of a chair and had to be sawed free. Nobby was always accident-prone!

Still, even though United weren't 'my team' I was pretty keyed up for the trial, which took place at the headquarters of the Lancashire County Football Association, St Bede's College, Manchester. I walked in on my own – Mr Davies had said my father could come, too, but Dad said he'd leave it to me – and I was dumbfounded to be introduced to none other than the famous Matt Busby, who was flanked by his assistant Jimmy Murphy, and chief coach Bert Whalley. It staggered me that such important and busy men would turn up for a kids' game, but later I was to learn that was exactly the kind of scrupulous attention to detail which was to pay handsome dividends for Manchester United.

I played the whole game out of position at wing-half and my main emotion was amazement at the high standard of the other players. I was convinced that there were so many good ones that I would not be wanted. My impression was that I had fared reasonably okay but without setting the world on fire and there could be no chance of going further, but after the game Jimmy Murphy and Bert Whalley asked me to sign amateur forms. So I was walking on air as I departed the beautiful playing fields of St Bede's. My future at Old Trafford was not exactly mapped out, but at least it seemed there were genuine grounds for hope.

However, in the short term there was disillusion in store. I went back to Whiston Youth Club, expecting to receive a further summons pretty soon, but nothing happened. Three months went by and I was certain they didn't want me after all, though George Davies always maintained that United's interest must have been genuine.

By then, unknown to my family, I was working in a coal mine. I had got to learn a certain amount about the industry through helping Dad with his work as union secretary over the years. He used to return home from meetings and ask me to do a lot of the writing for him, putting together the minutes and so on. So I knew that I could make some decent money in the pit – far more than anything I'd known before – and on my own initiative I enlisted at Lea Green colliery.

For a full six months, he thought I was doing odd jobs around the villages, and he found out the truth only when the miners went on strike. Then one of his mates, who knew what I was up to, asked him how his son was coping during the industrial action. Now Dad was a pretty easy-going fellow by nature but, without going mad, he was considerably more forceful than usual when telling me that he thought I had more sense than to go down the pit. But even though he didn't exactly agree with what I'd done, I think he was pleased that I had shown my independence, and at least he had found out that I could look after myself.

I had a close relationship with my father, there was a very strong bond with him, but we weren't of a type to be all over each other. He had finished his football career with New Brighton before he married my mother, Ruth, who was 12 years younger than him. Certainly myself and my two little sisters, Lily (three years younger) and Josephine (ten years younger) enjoyed an extremely contented childhood and I can't recall either parent ever being aggressive with me. My father never laid a hand on me in punishment, and if Mum got ratty she would do no more than give me a push.

But although Dad was essentially an equable soul, and an extremely popular figure on the local sports scene, he did not lack steel as he demonstrated vividly on the day that he reached the final of the Warrington Infirmary Invitation bowls competition. His opponent was a fellow named WH Frost, who had played as a full-back for Preston North End. This was an important event, which carried a prize of £100, a vast sum in those days, and it attracted heavy betting. My father took a seemingly decisive lead of 39 ends to 28 and there were plenty of wagers on him to win, but Frost knew that Dad suffered poor eyesight thanks to many years of pit work, so his tactics were to play from corner to corner, which is a considerable distance. My father just couldn't see that far and, on this occasion, he could not manage to roll one short, which would have been the answer.

Now so usual was it for Dad to win matches that, when he lost, then people who had placed money on him would shout that the match was fixed. Of course, it never was; he was a true sportsman and would never have stooped so low. But on this afternoon one barracker, who obviously had a substantial sum at risk, became particularly obnoxious as Frost crept back into contention. I knew that he was spouting nonsense, and could see plainly that my father was trying his utmost, but the fellow just refused to shut his mouth. Eventually Frost pulled back to 39-38 using the long mark, but finally

Dad managed to set him a short one from the corner to the crown. Coming off a long mark, which entails almost hurling the woods, it needs exceedingly fine judgment to bowl short again but my father managed it, getting two touches to win the game after all. That was unforgettable enough, but what happened next is etched even more indelibly on my memory.

The moment the game was finished, even before he was presented with his prize and the trophy, Dad took off his flat cap and strode purposefully across the green in search of his tormentor. When he spotted him, he marched up to the unfortunate fellow and struck him hard with his cap, calling him all the names under the sun. Then he lifted him up and shook him, before putting him down with a flourish. It seemed to me that the loud-mouthed spectator had got exactly what he deserved and yet, later, my father was forced to apologise. Nevertheless, his point had been well and truly made.

Throughout his life Dad worked hard, was straight in all his dealings, loved his sport and was a devoted family man. He died when he was in his middle seventies, having never been the same person after losing my mother to cancer when she was in her fifties. He had seemed to be in fine physical condition himself but when she died he seemed to give up. I suppose I've deviated from my tale a little here, but I make no apology because I feel a man's relationship with his father can offer a telling insight into his own character. Suffice it to say that I saw much of myself in Dad.

Getting back to my fledgling United career, it seemed to be withering even before it had a chance to flourish. I heard nothing from Old Trafford for several months after my so-called successful trial and really I thought that was the end of it. At that point I was approached by St Helens Town, a semi-professional club in the Lancashire Combination, which played to quite a high standard. In fact, an apt illustration of their quality is the fact that Bert Trautmann had performed for them in the season before he joined Manchester City, and he went on to become one of the truly great goalkeepers. For all that, I was a bit doubtful because I had signed papers for

United and was wary of doing anything illegal. However, I was assured it would be all right and the Town paid me £6 per win and £5 when we lost, which was a lot of money when I was earning pretty well from my mining job and professional football wages were hardly handsome at the time.

St Helens had a fantastic centre-half, an experienced former pro named Bill Twist, and I slotted in alongside him at right-half, managing to score a few goals. One time we played against Bolton Wanderers 'B' and after we had thrashed them, the chap in charge of their side asked me if I'd be interested in going to Burnden Park. It was my second approach from the Trotters and I was quite keen, but I told them about my earlier agreement with United and he promised to get in touch with Old Trafford to see what the situation was. Within about four days I received a letter from United asking me to turn up at their training ground, The Cliff, to represent their 'A' team. Obviously, until getting a reminder from their Lancashire rivals they had forgotten all about Bill Foulkes. On such little matters do whole careers hinge; there is so much luck involved with the way you progress. I could so easily have ended up at Burnden, though I'm not complaining; after all, had I done so it seems unlikely that I would ever have reached a European Cup Final.

By then, back in real life as you might call it, I had finished my surface training at the pit and then went below ground to work as a haulier. Often there were trucks which fell off the lines and they employed fellows with iron bars to lift them back on. I was obsessed with being super fit and strong for sport – that's something which never left me throughout my life – and so I used to lift these things back on to the tracks by hand, not bothering with the bars. They were extremely heavy and it was hard physical graft for a boy but I truly believe it stood me in good stead, building up muscles where I didn't even know I had muscles.

After a while, though, my supervisor asked me to train as an assistant manager, which was progress, a real step up in the world. If I had followed it through I could have ended up in charge of a coal face, a very responsible position. True, it took me away from heavy physical work and my physique suffered a bit, but I was better off financially and by then I was training twice a week with Manchester United anyway. So I found I had more money and more energy. Suddenly, for this footballing mineworker, life was looking very good, indeed.

# Three

## A double life

I HAD NO clear idea of it at the time, but when I started life as a Manchester United player, as a callow 18-year-old in 1950, I was a humble component on the richest production line of soccer talent ever seen in these islands. It was the dawning of the glorious but all-too-short era of the Busby Babes, and I was privileged to be a part of it.

My first appearance for the Red Devils was at right-half in the 'A' team in a Manchester League game at The Cliff and, with all due modesty, I wasn't out of my depth. In fact, I felt I was used to a higher standard with St Helens Town in the Lancashire Combination. I was strong and well-built, well used to bodily contact through all my Rugby League experience, I could get up to head the ball and if I wasn't all that fast, I wasn't all that slow, either. I used to love it when I was given a chance at centre-half and could have done with being a couple of inches taller, though I was no weakling. All the programmes used to list me at 5ft 11$\frac{1}{2}$ ins and 12 stone something, but actually I was 6ft (really I was!) and never less than 13$\frac{1}{2}$ stone. There was tremendous competition for places with four men's teams and at least three for youths, but I went straight into the men's game because I could handle it physically.

At first I was facing opposition such as Droylsden, Hyde United and Leek Town, plus the 'A' teams from Football League clubs such as Manchester City, Bolton and Preston North End. As I settled in, playing for the reserves as well as the 'A' team, I began to notice other names on the match programmes, the likes of Dennis Viollet, Mark Jones, Roger Byrne, Jeff Whitefoot and Eddie Lewis, all footballers who would win their spurs in the not-too-distant future.

It was clear by my progress that the management saw something in me even though every other player, to the very last man, could beat me technically. I was no fool and could see this, so I thought my only chance was to do exactly what Jimmy Murphy and the rest told me. That was my maxim: listen properly and then act on the advice with 100 per-cent determination. It was probably quite a rare outlook for a youngster, but always I was a realist and never tried to be fancy. I left that to others who were better qualified. I understood that every successful team needs a blend of contrasting attributes, and so I concentrated on my own physical strengths while the coaches worked on my positional play and ball technique.

By the time I reached the reserves I was at right-back, the berth in which I would enjoy all my pre-Munich success. I suppose with Mark Jones on the rise, they were already well-served at centre-half, my favourite position, but I was only too happy to be in the team wherever I was picked. That said, I never liked right-back, where I felt a little exposed, even though there weren't many wingers who gave me a chasing.

At one point, it must have been 1950/51, there arose what might have been a radical change in direction when Matt Busby and Jimmy Murphy instructed Bert Whalley to give me a run at centre-forward for the reserves. In retrospect, perhaps, a lot of people might be dumbfounded to imagine me leading the attack, but it was not such an alien concept in those days. I had scored plenty of goals for Whiston in open-age football and, given a smattering of opportunities for United's 'A' team, I found the net in every game. Then I headed the only goal in the final of the Gilchryst Cup against Leek Town in front of around 10,000 supporters at The Cliff, in what was my first ever game under floodlights. So, with the great Jack Rowley both injured and ageing, the Old Trafford regime was examining its long-term spearhead options through me, even though I had never even played for the first team.

When I lined up for the reserves I was spoilt, really, because I was playing between two outstanding inside-forwards, John Doherty and Johnny Downie. They were brilliant passers, usually delivering along the ground and with perfect weight. Such was their artistry that invariably they would put the ball into space for me. I didn't have to go smashing through people to reach it; all I had to do was run on to it and shoot. In this way I scored about 16 goals, including four in one game at Newcastle, and as a result I was chosen at number nine in a trial match between first team and reserves.

Now this was no gentle run-out because my immediate opponent was the veteran stopper Allenby Chilton, one of the toughest centre-halves who ever lived. I was a yard quicker than him at that stage of his career and managed to give him a hard time, scoring both goals as the reserves won 2-0. I was first to the ball most of the time and found I could resist him physically, which he didn't like at all. It was all B***** this and F*** that as he tried his best to intimidate me. But, my God, how he impressed me, even if he was past his very best. Despite having played hundreds of games and being comfortably the wrong side of 30, still he went for every ball as if his very life depended on it. Still he was consumed by the raw desire to win, making me realise how he had remained such a great player for so long.

The upshot of my personal performance was that Matt Busby called me up for a first-team debut away to West Bromwich Albion. However, it all went wrong for me in a practice session at The Cliff on the Thursday when Mark Jones and I went up for a header. Big Mark was pretty unbeatable in the air but, doubtlessly straining every sinew to impress, I landed awkwardly and tore ligaments in my ankle. As a result I was out for several months and had missed my chance to be a centre-forward. What with the subsequent arrival of the fabulous Tommy Taylor from Barnsley, it is hardly surprising that it never came again.

At the time it was a galling setback for a young fellow struggling as hard as I knew how to juggle the demands of two employers, the National Coal Board and Manchester United. While other reserves played football while perhaps fitting in a relatively unrigorous part-time job, I found I was stretched to the limit. On a typical day I would leave my bed at about 5 am, then walk across several fields to reach the colliery an hour later. Then I would do my shift, which admittedly by that time involved more administrative work than physical graft, and be up from undergound on the first winding of the cage at 2.30 pm. Then, on at least two days each week, I would shower at the pithead, snatch my football kit from my locker and catch a train from Lea Green station, arriving in Manchester at 4.30 pm, though training didn't start until 6 pm.

Because of my 'other life' I was a virtual stranger to most of the footballers, even though I had been there for three years when I reached the fringe of the first team. The only times I saw most of them were for matches on Saturdays and the twice-weekly training sessions, which meant I was never 'one of the lads.' In the circumstances I was grateful to Dennis Viollet, who also had a part-time job and who occasionally used to take me to a bar after our training session. He was a real character who lived life to the full, as they say, and I was never in his class as a socialite. Another fellow who helped me enormously was Laurie Cassidy, the reserves' centre-forward, who made his living as a schoolmaster. He was a lovely man, an understanding character in whom I could confide, and he was a huge help to my career. He managed only four games at senior level but he was a fantastic influence on the youngsters in the second string. Laurie went on to succeed as a headmaster in Manchester and no one could have deserved it more. Also part-time was Billy Redman, a very quick full-back who earned a title medal in 1951/52 but who never became fully established. He went on to be a successful businessman and even in those days he was a company director who earned much more money outside football than in it.

After training I tended to catch the 10.15 pm train from Manchester Exchange back home to Rainhill or on to Liverpool, where I often snatched some time with my future wife, Teresa. That meant that I wouldn't be home until way after midnight, then had to be up again by five the next morning. I did that for several years and it was no way for a professional athlete to live, but I was very young and very fit at the time.

I have been a fitness fanatic all my life and on nights when there were no United sessions, often I would train at Charlie Fox's gym in St Helens. I used to push myself to the limit to build myself up and he used to reckon I might have made it as a boxer, such was the power of my right hook on the punchbags. I was always going for extra runs, too, desperate for that last ounce of fitness, utterly determined to pull out every last stop in an attempt to make the grade at football.

I just wanted it so much, not for the money because there was next to none of that in the game at the time. I went to the pit to pay for my keep. No, it was for its own sake, something I had to do. I felt all this strength and vitality and energy in my body and I wanted to do something constructive with it. Knowing that the rest of the United players were technically superior only spurred me on to more intense efforts. I knew I must impose myself physically to stand the slightest chance, and I developed my own method of combating bigger opponents, especially in the air. At the moment of springing, I would climb up their calves, effectively using them as a launchpad. Some people might think that's in my imagination, but I can assure them it's not. How do they think I kept on top of the giant Portuguese Jose Torres in the 1968 European Cup Final? It would have been physically impossible for me to dominate such a big man by any other means. I had to have a knack, an edge, a method, call it what you will. I admit that I used my opponent, and it was a part of my game for which I do not apologise. In fact, I relished it.

But I don't want to make out that I rose through United's ranks by violence, far from it. If I had a secret it was dedication, and anyway I would not have got far at Old Trafford by trying to come over as a hard case. There were too many genuinely flinty characters, such as the aforementioned Mr Chilton, for me to have got away with that.

I have unending admiration for the seasoned professionals I encountered when I arrived at Old Trafford, the men who made up Matt Busby's first breathtakingly attractive team in the years immediately after the Second World War. What impressed so much, apart from their magnificence on the football field, was their camaraderie. They were extremely close-knit, a real unit, and I could draw a ready parallel to life down a coal mine. At first when you went underground, the other men would be mere faces, but after a time you would come to know them and, more important, to rely on them. That's what it was like at Manchester United and I believe it was an ethos which stemmed from Matt Busby, who himself hailed from a humble pitman's cottage in the Lanarkshire mining village of Orbiston. He understood basic values and possessed this incredible ability to mould men together into teams. Three times he achieved that at Old Trafford: immediately after the war, then again during the 1950s and, most amazing of all, yet again in the wake of the Munich calamity.

Of his first team, centre-half Allenby Chilton stands out particularly prominently in my memory, perhaps because of our early encounter. He was an awkward, testy fellow who often picked an argument and was known to chin a few people – and yet he was loved. There is no better word for the regard in which he was held at the club. People used to accept his occasional outbursts with 'Oh, it's Allenby, that's the way he is!' Above all he was a leader who inspired by example and who was afraid of absolutely nothing. Allenby Chilton was a prodigiously strong man, and that tends to define his image, but also he was a much more accomplished footballer than he was given credit for. In the air he was majestic and, in his prime, he was pretty well unbeatable on the ground, too. He won only two England caps, which was an insult to a player of his stature, but in the days before the England manager was allowed to pick the team, he fell victim to the ridiculous whims of an international selection panel drawn from the clubs. It was alleged that there was corruption, that club representatives used to push their own players just to increase their value on the transfer market, and I can well believe it.

Another awkward so-and-so was centre-forward Jack Rowley, known universally as 'The Gunner' in reference to his ferocious shot. Jack was rarely polite to anyone, but with me he was fine, and if ever he was a bit abrasive I never took offence because I could see he didn't mean it. He'd say: 'Foulkesy, how are you son?' He was the first to call me Foulkesy, and getting a nickname from such an influential person meant a lot to me. Mind, it was best to be on the right side of Jack as he illustrated during a break at Harrogate, prior to playing Huddersfield during my early days at the club. Having just completed a shift at the mine, I joined the rest of the players in a hotel lounge as they were waiting for Matt to look in for his team talk. There was quite a lively conversation, during which Jack told Reg Allen, the big 'keeper, that he didn't know what the hell he was talking about, that he was bloody mad. Reg leapt up and hit Jack so hard that he shot over the back of a settee. Reg was striding round the furniture to give him some more and Jack was squaring up for a battle when everybody grabbed them, pulling them apart. I wondered whether such disturbances happened often, and I was told they were not rare. Rowley's rudeness was cited as a frequent cause, along with Allen's volatile disposition and a tendency for Chilton to be, shall we say, a little bit naughty at times! But for all Jack's rough edges, there was no denying that he could score goals as easily as if he was shelling peas. Even in 1954/55, his last season at United when he was in his middle thirties, I remember an FA Cup thunderbolt against Reading which the goalkeeper must not even have seen.

As for Reg Allen, I was to discover from personal experience that you crossed him at your peril. One afternoon when I had been given time off by the Coal Board to train with United in the university grounds at Fallowfield, we were having a kick-in with Reg between the posts. He was looking elsewhere as I sent in a shot and the ball caught him full in the face. It was totally inadvertent but there was no way this hot-tempered fellow was going to wait for an apology from young Bill Foulkes. He just turned and glared, and I had never seen such a murderous look in any man's eyes. There was nothing for it but to take to my heels and he chased me out of the ground, up the main road to a big roundabout at the top, all around that and back down the road to the training pitch. He was a big, muscular guy but fortunately I was fitter than he was and he couldn't catch me. If he had I don't think I'd have lived to be writing this now!

In marked contrast to the turbulent Rowley was his frontline partner, Stan Pearson, a lovely footballer and an absolute gentleman. Stan was a magnificent inside-forward, a maker and taker of goals, both a beautifully subtle passer and a truly predatory finisher. In addition he was a terrific help to all the youngsters flooding into Old Trafford at the time – as, to be fair, was Jack Rowley. At some clubs the senior players frowned on the kids, seeing them as potential threats to their future employment in an era when there was little cash to be made from playing football, but Pearson and company could not have been more generous with their time and expertise.

Another like that was Johnny Carey, our Irish skipper and one of the classiest operators, whether at right-back or right-half, it has ever been my privilege to see. When I played behind him for the first time, making my senior debut against Liverpool at Anfield in December 1952, he looked like an old guy; prematurely balding, a bit stooped, shorts too long for him, he didn't seem anything like the popular idea of a professional athlete. But he didn't take long to open my eyes, just strolling through the action, intercepting and prompting, always cool and always in control. Though he was way past his best and seemed to have difficulty in running, he remained superb in the air, just flicking balls unerringly to the feet of team-mates, and I left the pitch thanking my lucky stars to have played alongside such a master. I learned so much from that guy in the course of just one game.

I hold the rest of Matt's first wonderful team in high regard, too, such players as dynamic wing-half Henry Cockburn, accomplished full-back John Aston – whose son, also John, would play such a thrilling part in our European Cup triumph of 1968 – and the reliable goalkeeper Jack Crompton, even though he used to cuss me at times when I first got in the team and did some silly things through inexperience. Then there was outside-left Charlie Mitten, arguably the finest of all uncapped wingers, who left the club soon after I arrived; he was seeking a crock of gold in Colombia, one which failed sadly to materialise. The famous 48-ers, as they will be known forever because of that year's sensational FA Cup Final triumph over Blackpool, were completed by doughty wing-half John Anderson, and the brilliant right-wing pair of Jimmy Delaney and Johnny Morris, all of whom I had little or no experience of playing alongside.

Thus I learned my trade under the influence of impeccable role models and I had completed a comprehensive grounding when the time came to step into first-team action that afternoon at Liverpool. That was a landmark for which I had yearned for so long, and it turned out to be especially daunting as, in all honesty, I wasn't really fit at the time. I was recovering from an ankle injury suffered in training when I was called into Matt Busby's office, and I feared the worst. I hadn't the slightest inkling of an imminent call-up and, with so many splendid players at the club, it crossed my mind that the boss was about to dispense with my services.

But as I walked in he seemed cheerful and questioned me about my ankle; apparently he knew there was a problem and he wanted to see for himself, so he asked me to jump as high as I could, right there in front of his desk. I did so and, when I landed with a slight grimace, he said: 'How was that?' Well, in truth the pain was killing me, but there was no way I would admit to it, so I replied: 'Okay'. He smiled and said he thought he'd play me on Saturday against Liverpool, and I assumed he meant in the reserves at Old Trafford. Then he mentoned about me living in the St Helens area and that I might as well meet the team at the ground. I thought he must have been mistaken and pointed out that the first team were playing at Anfield. He replied: 'Yes, you're in the first team.' I could have fallen through the floor and barely heard what he added about my expenses being paid. All I could think of saying was 'thank you', then I just went. I was in a dream, so excited that I couldn't focus properly on anything. Later I pondered on my white lie, and wondered how wise I had been, but I believed genuinely that I could be fit in time, and I would never have put the team in jeopardy by making a wildly false claim about my condition. In any case, Matt was a shrewd and experienced operator, and although he didn't let on, I'm certain he knew the score.

My opportunity had arisen during a period of change. United were the reigning champions but were lagging behind the League leaders and the boss was in the process of revitalising the team with youngsters. There was a flu epidemic, too, which claimed right-back Tommy McNulty and opened the door for me. My immediate opponent was the revered Billy Liddell, who was easily Liverpool's most important player. An indication of his stature was that he and Stanley Matthews were the only two men to be selected for Great Britain against the Rest of Europe in both 1947 and 1955, so it's pretty clear that when I ran up against him in 1952 he was at his peak. He was renowned for his pace and his power as well as exceptional skill, but he was one of nature's gentlemen, too, and I could not have wished for better treatment from him. He knew I was making my debut and he was very kind to me before kick-off, finding a moment to say: 'I wish you all the very best, son.' Momentarily that made me feel rather churlish because a few seconds earlier, as I had gazed at the Anfield idol I had vowed that I would not be overawed and muttered to myself: 'If he hits me I'll break his bloody neck!'. Of course, even after his thoughtful remark, Billy did his best to take me apart because that was his job, and he gave me a very thorough examination. But although he lost me once, putting Liverpool ahead after just ten minutes, I stuck to my task and we came back to win through goals from John Aston and Stan Pearson. I admit that I was worried after we conceded our goal, but Johnny Carey did an archetypal elder statesman's job in keeping me on an even keel. He told me to keep on doing the simple things well and we would prevail – and so it proved. I was lucky to have Johnny playing in front of me at right-half, because he shielded me from Liddell to a large extent, making timely interceptions to cut off his supply of the ball. Afterwards the captain came up to me and asked my age. I told him I was 20, he looked me in the eye and declared, in that soft Irish brogue of his: 'I think you'll do well'. That's all it was, nothing over the top to turn a young fellow's head, but it made me feel 8ft tall.

For myself, I thought I'd done okay without being anything special. I suppose I clobbered Billy Liddell a few times, not trying to kick him but making fair tackles, and I was quietly satisfied that I had got to the ball before such an illustrious opponent on several occasions. Matt Busby said nothing to me about my performance but he must have been pleased because he told me to get ready for the next first-team game, which was against Chelsea at Stamford Bridge a week later.

Already, though, there was a cloud on my horizon. As I left Anfield my suspect ankle was extremely sore and I decided against limping to the train station, instead taking a taxi straight to the Liverpool home of Teresa, my fiancee. By the time I hobbled through the door I was in agony and her family gathered round to have a look at it. It was horribly swollen and Teresa's father, who reckoned I had no chance of playing again in seven days time, hurried me to the local hospital, where it was packed with ice, all without any reference to the club. Somehow I managed to get through training that week and started the Chelsea game, but by half-time I could barely walk, let alone run. Matt could see that I couldn't cope and, as there were no substitutes back then, he moved me to centre-forward which enabled the versatile John Aston – who had been filling in for the injured Jack Rowley – to return to his specialist position of full-back. Given the state I was in I could only potter around up front, but I managed one meaningful touch when a loose ball fell to me; I couldn't use my best foot so I whipped it with my left, it crashed against the bar and rebounded to John Doherty, who scored. We won 3-2, so at least I felt I had made some contribution, though it was to be my last of the season. The ankle really was in a bad way and I was not back in contention until 1953/54.

# Four

# Meet the Babes

IN THE early 1950s, Manchester United were in the grip of a transition the like of which no club had been through before, and I doubt seriously whether quite such a seismic eruption will ever happen again. Matt Busby's first great team, which had won the FA Cup so breathtakingly in 1948, was beginning to break up, and even though the League title was finally captured after a series of near-misses in 1951/52, certainly the old guard was on its way out.

It was such an exciting time at Old Trafford. Youngsters were surging in on an endless wave of talent, flocking from all over the country. You didn't know where to look because all of a sudden there would be yet another brilliant newcomer and none of them riveted the eye like one lad from Dudley, name of Duncan Edwards. When I first bumped into Duncan at The Cliff and they told me he was only 15, I simply couldn't believe it. He had a man's body, a giant's really, although he had the face of a boy. He was so mature in terms of his football and his physique, with all the natural ability anyone could ever imagine. Every time he did something, on the training pitch or in a match, he would surprise me. Despite his massive muscular stature, this man-mountain could bring off the most delicate of manoeuvres. When he wanted to be he was all flicks and swivels, almost like a conjuror, and it seemed that he could stun the ball dead with practically any part of his anatomy. But unlike some players, his tricks were not window dressing, they were related directly to game situations. Duncan could drive the ball accurately over vast distances with either foot, he could coax short passes through the eye of a needle, he could send an opponent the wrong way with the sweetest of swerves. For all that, though, what really took the breath away was his sheer power. He was awesome in the air and on the deck people would just bounce off him. West Bromwich Albion's Maurice Setters, later to become an Old Trafford team-mate of mine, was a formidably abrasive individual, and I recall him threatening Duncan, who was in the act of taking a throw-in. Maurice was positively bristling with aggression, but our boy just shot him a contemptuous glance, stuck out his chest and poor Maurice was sent reeling. For all the apparent effort Duncan put into that slight movement, he might have been brushing off a fly.

I've never seen a perfect player, not even George Best was that, but if my arm was twisted I'd have to say that the nearest to perfection I have seen was Duncan Edwards. So superb was he that it was difficult to nail down his best position. Usually he played at left-half, bolstering the defence and commanding the midfield, but sometimes, in an emergency, he would be thrown into attack and I have seen him transform games as a centre-forward.

Yet despite all his attributes, and the fact that he became a national institution while still in his teens, he was a steady, down-to-earth lad. Oh, I think he knew he was special and he carried a certain quiet confidence, but there wasn't an ounce of conceit about him. Certainly he didn't bask in the limelight, rather he would shun it, preferring a quiet evening with his girlfriend to a night on the razzle. Generally Duncan was imperturbable, exactly what might be expected of a gentle giant, and I never saw him rattled throughout our half-dozen or so years together at Old Trafford. The only time I ever saw him shaken was during his National Service, when he was in the Army team which I captained. He didn't like the regimentation, what he saw as the petty discipline, of life in the forces and, though he never made a song and dance about it, he railed against it in private. Because of who he was, there was always someone trying to bring him down, to make life difficult for him, and he told me: 'I'll be bloody glad to get out of this, the sooner the better!' It was different for me, I enjoyed Army life on the whole, but then I wasn't a celebrity like Duncan and was left substantially to my own devices.

Another wing-half, but offering a vivid contrast in personality, was Eddie Colman. As gregarious as Duncan was retiring, Eddie was at the centre of every social occasion. If anyone was going to leap on stage and sing, then it would be the ebullient little fellow from Salford, and he had a fantastic sense of humour, too. I was a hulking great brute alongside him, but if United were going away he would tell Teresa: 'Don't worry about Bill, I won't let anyone touch him, I'll take care of him for you!' Eddie was a great one for music and he took his record player with him everywhere we went. He loved Louis Armstrong and Frank Sinatra in particular, and even today when I hear those wonderful performers, it whisks me back in my mind to the Norbreck Hotel in Blackpool, where we used to prepare for big games. Eddie used to get his records from Barry Kelsall's shop at the end of Deansgate, next to the Exchange railway station in central Manchester. That place was like a social club to us. Perhaps half a dozen of us would drop in and Barry, who became a firm friend, would play us all sorts of music, from the latest pop to modern jazz. Eddie was always to the forefront of that crowd, always wanting to be up with the latest trends.

Like Duncan, he was only 21 when he died at Munich, but unlike the big man he never played for his country. Had he lived, though, international caps would have been a certainty because, even though he was only a tot, he was a fabulous footballer. Passing was his speciality, he reached his target with practically every ball he delivered, and he was a sharp tackler, while he was christened 'Snakehips' by the press in tribute to his mesmeric body-swerve. In fact, Harry Gregg reckoned that when Eddie swayed, he did it so persuasively that the girders on the grandstand swayed with him! I got on well with all the lads who lost their lives in the tragedy, but I had a specially soft spot for Eddie Colman.

Having spoken of Duncan and Eddie, who spring into my mind whenever anyone mentions the Busby Babes, I'll go on to record my impressions of the other members of that unique team. Actually, I should say two teams, because Matt had gathered about him more than 20 fine young players of such exceptional quality that by the mid 1950s I believe United could have fielded two sides capable of finishing in the First Division's top six.

The man in on-field charge of this once-in-a-lifetime collection was left-back Roger Byrne, who was a little older than the rest of the boys and had picked up a title medal in 1951/52. Matt had converted him from a left-winger and his past as a forward was evident in his terrific speed and his lovely left foot, even though it should be said that he could barely head a ball to save his life. Clean-cut and upright, Roger was a born leader, and though he wasn't captain when we first met, I always thought he would be the natural successor to Johnny Carey. Extremely intelligent, utterly straight and radiating self-confidence without being arrogant, he was forthright in his views and many of the players were wary of his sharp tongue, but he was good-hearted and a trusty friend to me. In my part-time days, when I had no particularly close pals at the club, after a training session he would take me into town for a meal, often at a Chinese restaurant. We'd chat not only about the game – although certainly he gave me a comprehensive insight into what it took to be a professional foot-baller – but also about every subject under the sun. It was an education in itself listening to Roger, who seemed far more sophisti-cated than most people in the game.

Sure, he could he hot-headed when he had a bee in his bonnet, and he had his disagreements with the manager, who once almost sent him home from a tour of the USA. But Matt wanted a strong character to be his skipper, a man who commanded respect from his colleagues, kept himself in tip-top shape and who understood the game thoroughly. Clearly he found him in Roger Byrne, who had won 33 successive England caps by the time he perished at Munich. But for the accident I am sure he would have emerged as the ideal long-term replacement for Billy Wright as captain of his country.

One telling measure of Roger's all-round excellence was the fact that he kept out of the team such a capable performer as his fellow Mancunian Geoff Bent. The former skipper of both Salford and England Schoolboys, Geoff was quick, skilful and hard, and surely would have walked into any other side in the country. I remember taking Teresa to her first football match, when I was in the reserves, and asking afterwards what she had thought of my display. She replied: 'Oh, you were very good. Nobody could get past that number-three shirt.' That sounded fine, except that I had been playing at right-back and she had been concentrating on Geoff all afternoon. Like me, he was tall and slim with curly hair, so I suppose it was an understandable mistake. That was Teresa's excuse anyway! Had he lived, instead of dying alongside Roger on that horrific afternoon at Munich, it is difficult to believe that such a classy performer would have remained in the shadows indefinitely.

While discussing defenders, let me say that I would have liked to have occupied the centre of the rearguard myself, as it was always my favoured position, but Matt used me at right-back in those days and the number-five shirt was contested by Mark Jones and Jackie Blanchflower. Illustrating the fantastic spirit in the squad, the pair of them were close chums, even though they became fierce rivals for a place. When Allenby Chilton bowed out in 1955 it seemed a sure bet that Mark would succeed him, and so he did for a time, with Jackie featuring frequently as a goal-scoring inside-forward. But then Matt converted the Ulsterman into a centre-half and thereafter, until the air disaster intervened, first one of them held sway and then the other.

They offered a huge contrast in styles, Mark being a traditionally commanding bulwark and Jackie a far more cultured footballer. Personally I prefer my central stoppers in the Jones mould, big, strong and dominating, the sort of figure to build a defence around. Yorkshireman Mark was a really lovely fellow, a decent family man, but my word he was a tough nut, and nobody took liberties with him either on or off the field. At the time of the crash he was in the team and, having performed majestically in helping United to overcome Red Star Belgrade in the quarter-finals of the European Cup, he looked set to remain there. That said Jackie, an Irish charmer, was a formidable adversary, a delightfully smooth operator adept at timing interceptions and passing his way out of trouble. There were times when he lost possession in dicey situations, but overall he was extremely accomplished and offered a fascinatingly different option. Who would have prevailed in the long run? Well, Mark was just starting to demonstrate the full extent of his prowess, while Jackie positively oozed class. Of course, Mark was killed and Jackie was maimed on that damned runway, so we shall never know.

Another outstanding Busby Babe who often tends to be forgotten, at least by Old Trafford outsiders, was Jeff Whitefoot. He was a thoroughbred wing-half, a beautiful passer who had joined the club in his early teens and grew up in the Manchester United way. Eventually he lost out to Eddie Colman and moved on, first to Grimsby Town and then to Nottingham Forest, whom he helped to win the FA Cup in 1959, but I was always sad about his departure. Any top club needed more than 11 players, then as now, and it was a pity that Jeff was not persuaded to stay. After Munich there were rumours that he might re-sign, and when assistant boss Jimmy Murphy mentioned it to me I told him it was a marvellous idea, but it never happened.

And so to the forwards, a department in which the new Manchester United were opulently blessed. Dennis Viollet, Tommy Taylor, Billy Whelan, Johnny Berry, David Pegg, Bobby Charlton, Albert Scanlon, Kenny Morgans, John Doherty … the list is unsurpassable by any other British club.

I'll start with Dennis, whom I maintain to be one of the most underrated footballers in the club's history, a goal-grabbing inside-forward who possessed the potential to become an all-time great. He had everything – flair, skill, pace, intelligence, courage – and it seemed incomprehensible to me that England searched in vain for a suitable partner for Tommy Taylor, and yet the right man was playing alongside him, week in and week out, for Manchester United. The selectors must have been idiots never to try them as a pair at international level, opting instead for people who, with all due respect, were carthorses in comparison. Taylor and Viollet operated as if by telepathy, the one invariably knowing the whereabouts and intentions of the other. It was such a common sight for Tommy to soar above defenders and knock the ball down to the feet of Dennis, and even more frequently Dennis would create space by a subtle run, allowing Tommy to slash in yet another goal.

Amazingly Dennis was even more prolific after the disaster which claimed his sidekick's life, yet he was not capped until May 1960, at the end of a season in which he had netted 32 times in the League, which remains a United record to this day. Not too long afterwards, though he was still the right side of 30, he was sold to Stoke City which, even with David Herd on the scene and Denis Law on the horizon, always seemed regrettable to me. Perhaps Old Trafford was getting a trifle crowded in the strikers' department, but there is always room for a player of Dennis Viollet's calibre at any club.

As for Tommy Taylor, if I was asked to describe him in two words, I would say, simply: the greatest. That he was the finest all-round centre-forward of his day, there is not the slightest shadow of a doubt. In the air he had no contemporary peer, nobody had a chance against him, and judges I respect have even compared him to Tommy Lawton, renowned as the most brilliant header of a ball in the game's history. On the ground, too, Tommy Taylor had the lot. He was a terrific athlete who could run with the ball and once he got into his stride he wouldn't be caught. His strength and stamina were limitless, so that he used to get on the end of passes which he had no right to reach. I used to feel sorry for the centre-halves who faced him, because he would run them into the ground, absolutely terrorising them throughout the 90 minutes. Sometimes, when I was under pressure in defence, I would just whack the ball down the channel, and who would be on the end of it, pretty well every time? Tommy

Taylor. Then he would shout 'Good pass, Bill' and I would thank him for the compliment, but deep down I'd know that it was only Tommy who had made it into a good ball. But he wasn't just a big bustler, he had far more skill then he was credited with, and often he would take the ball round the goalkeeper. By the time he died at Munich he had only just celebrated his 26th birthday and was getting better all the time. In my opinion, his peak wasn't even in sight, yet he had ousted Nat Lofthouse from the England side, and Nat was a long way from being a back number at that point. Tommy had scored 16 goals in 19 games for his country and might have expected at least another five years at the top. Like so many of the lads who never came home from Belgrade, there was no limit to what he would have achieved.

After joining United from Barnsley in the spring of 1953 for a fee of £29,999 – Matt was determined that the breezy young Yorkshireman would not have the pressure of a £30,000 price tag, so he gave the extra £1 to the tea lady – Tommy made himself at home at Old Trafford from the word go. Apart from scoring seven goals in his first eight games as the season drew to a close, thus signalling that the manager's lengthy search for a long-term successor to Jack Rowley was over at last, he proved immensely popular off the pitch, too. Tommy was everybody's pal but he was especially close to Jackie Blanchflower and the pair of them liked a beer or three, but there was nothing wrong with that. We all liked a drink in those days – certainly Jimmy Murphy did – but it was never taken to excess because we were all professionals, and no harm was done.

One of my most hair-raising memories of Tommy takes me back to a celebration at the Midland Hotel, in the centre of Manchester, after one of our European wins. At the end of the evening Teresa and I were hailing a taxi when Tommy, who lived not far from us in Sale, grinned: 'You don't have to bother with that, I'll give you a lift. I wasn't too sure because he could be a bit cavalier, to say the least, but Teresa thought it would be fun, so we went. True to character, Tommy put his foot down and soon we were approaching the roundabout at Trafford Bar pretty fast, rather too fast. As he attempted to negotiate the turn, he lost control, the car spun like a top and I thought: 'This is the end.' Miraculously, though, we didn't hit anything and we jumped out, relieved to be alive. Then, on asking a few pertinent questions, we discovered that he had no brakes, that it wasn't his car – he had borrowed it from a chum – and that he had no driving licence! On closer inspection, too, we saw that the car was a dilapidated old thing, so we declined his gleeful invitation to continue the journey and hailed a taxi. These days, of course, no England centre-forward would be banging around Manchester in a borrowed jalopy; he would be behind the wheel of a Ferrari, or a Lamborghini, or the like, but back in the 1950s very few footballers had cars at all. As a general rule we weren't allowed to drive, because of the possibility – should that be probability? – of accidents, but one of the few who did was Roger Byrne. He was a responsible type, and he needed transport because he was studying to be a physiotherapist and had to get to and from his courses. The club might have regretted making an exception, though, because one night Roger drove into Matt Busby's garden wall, pretty well demolishing it. Fortunately no one was injured. Eventually I think I was the second man to be allowed a car because I was living in Huyton, Liverpool, at the time, with some 30 miles each way to travel to work.

But we digress. Yet another outstanding member of the Busby Babes' attack was Liam 'Billy' Whelan, a sublimely skilful inside-right who was brought over from Dublin in 1953 and pitchforked into the FA Youth Cup Final as a replacement for poor John Doherty, who had suffered a serious knee injury. Billy could look slow on the pitch, moving with an awkward, ungainly gait, but he had stamina in abundance and I would guarantee that if the players went for a mile run, then he would be the first back every time. What made him special, though, was his mastery over the ball, which was quite phenomenal.

The match which epitomises his worth to me was the away leg of our European Cup quarter-final against Athletic Bilbao in January

1957. That night in Spain we were trailing 5-2 with only five minutes remaining, and it seemed that we were on our way out of the competition. But Billy picked up the ball on half-way, then seemed to float over a quagmire of a pitch that was half mud and half snow, beating a succession of defenders before shooting into the top corner from 25 yards. It was one of the most thrilling goals I ever witnessed, it restored our hope, and duly we won the tie. After that he did the same sort of thing on plenty of occasions, pulling off the seemingly impossible, roaming free and then rifling home from distance. Billy scored more than 50 times in fewer than 100 senior appearances for United, a fantastic record, and although he had lost his place to Bobby Charlton at the time of Munich, I am sure that, had he lived, he would have taken a major role in the club's future. I'm not saying he would have kept Bobby out in the long run – I don't think anyone could have done that – but somehow space would have been found for Billy more often than not.

As well as being a superb footballer, this softly-spoken Dubliner was one of the loveliest men I ever met, so modest and decent. He was very religious, too, with a certain tranquility about him, and sometimes he used to come out with sayings which made me think he might have been a priest. I was sitting near him as our plane attempted to take off for the third time on that fateful afternoon at Munich and I heard Billy say something along the lines of: 'If anything happens, then I'm ready for it.' With all the tension, with people scurrying around the aircraft as they changed seats, he was utterly calm. In that moment, it didn't really occur to me what he was talking about, but when I discussed it later with Teresa I realised. Billy was a devout Catholic, and he was preparing himself for the worst if it happened. What a character, and what a player, he would have become had he been spared.

The lad Billy had replaced some four and a half years earlier, John Doherty, was a fabulous performer, too, a cultured inside-forward who could pull off every trick in the book. He was blessed by a priceless combination of ability to burn and the intelligence to make the most of it, and it was a crying shame that a severe knee injury – which saw him invalided out of National Service – should prevent his full flowering at Old Trafford. However, it's to his enormous credit that, for all his fitness problems, he fought back to displace Billy Whelan for a spell and earn a Championship medal on merit in 1955/56. What spoke volumes for John's sheer class was that he always seemed to have time to do what he wanted with the ball. He could pull it down with a single touch, no matter how awkward the angle it came to him, he was a beautiful passer and he carried a ferocious shot. He was equally smooth off the pitch, too, a bit of a man about town; I'm sure he enjoyed himself to the full, and why not? Even in those days before footballers were as ludicrously high-profile as they are today, they were celebrities and life was sweet. It was different for me because I was so busy with my job down the mine, but the situation must have been enough to turn any young man's head.

I haven't mentioned the wingers, yet, and we were exceedingly well off in that department. Essentially there were four, Johnny Berry and Kenny Morgans who played on the right, and David Pegg and Albert Scanlon who contested the number-11 shirt. Of these, Johnny was rather a man apart, having arrived in Manchester from Birmingham City as a 25-year-old, and already an established top performer, back in 1951. Matt Busby had coveted him ever since the feisty little fellow had tormented United's defence on several occasions and was delighted to acquire him as a long-term replacement for Jimmy Delaney. Johnny could embark on thrillingly mazy dribbles, having the knack of cutting past opponents on either side, and could prove a thorn to any defence. Also he was remarkably tough for a winger and – unlike many flankmen in those days – he was willing to scrap for every ball. Johnny was like a cock bantam, and if he went into a scrimmage, it was unusual if he didn't come out on top. In truth, he could be an awkward customer off the field, too, very argumentative. Once, after drawing a game with Luton which we should have won, somebody in the dressing room demanded of Johnny why he hadn't cleared the ball when he'd had the chance. He reacted spikily and the next minute there was a free-for-all scrap, which was pretty well unknown among the Babes, who had engendered a magnificent team ethos. Then Matt came in and was furious with them. They knew that his policy was for no immediate recriminations, believing that any inquests should be left for a day or so until passions had cooled. Now, finding some of his players at each other's throats, he laced into them. I thought the whole thing rather amusing, but Matt didn't. Still, Johnny's fire was part of his all-round excellence as a performer. In addition, he packed a terrific shot for such a small person, being able to clout it savagely with either foot, and he was a superb crosser who supplied a great deal of the ammunition for Tommy Taylor. Also he was adept at switching positions with Tommy, frequently unhinging defences by popping up in the middle when least expected. He had reached his thirties and was out of the team at the time of the disaster, but such was his insatiable fighting spirit that I am sure we would not have seen the last of Johnny Berry had he not sustained injuries at Munich which ended his career.

That said, Kenny Morgans had ousted him and the bright young Welshman might not have been easy to elbow aside. Only 18 at the time of the crash, Kenny was enjoying an electric run of form, a consistently exciting all-round performer who, every now and then, brought out something truly special. Sadly, after the accident, even though he had escaped with superficial physical injuries, he was a ghost of his former self, never even coming close to his previous level. After a few frustratingly peripheral post-Munich outings for United, Kenny moved on, serving Swansea and Newport back in his homeland before retiring with so many possibilities unexplored. And that was overwhelmingly sad.

Over on the left flank, Matt Busby was spoilt for choice in the talented persons of David Pegg and Albert Scanlon. Both of them were marvellous footballers and they offered a total contrast in footballing styles. David, a lively, fun-loving lad from Doncaster – we had quite a colony of Yorkshiremen, what with Mark Jones and

Tommy Taylor – was a ball-player with delicate, silky control. No matter how muddy or icy the surface, he seemed to flow over it, and although he was a superb crosser, often he was at his most dangerous when he cut inside. David scored some lovely goals that way, but first and foremost he was a creator. Had he survived Munich I am convinced that he could have looked forward to plenty more England caps to add to the one he had received by the time of his death.

As for Albert, he was an out-and-out flyer, one of the most exciting orthodox wingers I have ever seen. Far more direct than David but without his intricate skills, he would beat defenders with a high-speed swerve followed by devastating acceleration. He attacked opponents head-on, he was very strong and he had a lethal left foot which dispatched some truly memorable goals. At the time of the air crash, in which Albert suffered a head injury which kept him out until the subsequent season, he had earned his place at David's expense and was enjoying the form of his life. When he came back in 1958/59 he continued to cut quite a dash and was more prolific as a goal-scorer than ever before, but then I believe he suffered a delayed reaction to the tragedy. Somehow a spark went out of his game and before long he had slipped away to Newcastle, which would have seemed unthinkable back in 1958. I missed Albert, an engaging local lad who was as sharp as a tack in his young days, a real live wire.

Which of the two left-wingers would have prevailed at Old Trafford in the long run? Impossible to say. Both had so much to offer that it would have benefited the club to keep the two, though I suppose that would have been unrealistic. At youth level Matt and Jimmy had solved the problem by playing David at inside-left, but with the plethora of talent available at senior level that would have been unlikely. It would have been an agonising conundrum for the Boss to solve. I only wish he'd had to make the choice.

That leaves only one major outfield player to mention, a certain Bobby Charlton, and I'll discuss him in more detail later, when examining United's fabulous team of the 1960s. But even back in the 1950s it was clear that the miner's son from Ashington in

Northumberland was something very special, indeed. Even in the midst of the mouth-watering array of talent which Matt Busby had assembled, he stood out as an absolute natural. Bobby might be having a quiet game, but then suddenly he would pop up with a sensational goal out of nothing, most likely a scorcher from 30 yards, or change the course of a match with a raking 40-yard pass. To me, strictly a journeyman footballer, the accuracy and weight of his passing over long distances verged on the uncanny. He knew instinctively whether to deliver to feet or into the path of a team-mate and he would do it instantly, which was practically impossible for the opposition to counter. But there was even more to Bobby than the making and taking of spectacular goals. He was a phenomenal athlete who had stamina in spades; an inside-forward in those days, he was up and down the pitch constantly, seeming to float over tackles, as graceful as a gazelle. Off the pitch, like me, he was quiet and, what with the pair of us sharing a mining background, I suppose I always felt a certain affinity for him. In addition, of course, we were brought closer by the crash. Before Munich, though, his best pals seemed to be Tommy Taylor and David Pegg. Together they were so funny, always laughing and joking. They didn't have a care in the world, and it showed. As a youngster Bobby was never the most punctual of individuals and I remember one morning when the team bus called for him at his digs, not far from the ground, and he came out shamefacedly, only half-dressed and with his hair all dishevelled (yes, he had some in those days!) His team-mates gave him a hard time for sleeping in, but he took it well. Certainly he was a shy lad when he first broke into the team and my wife Teresa – to whom you would never apply that description – remembers fondly an evening spent with Bobby, watching a beauty contest for which I was one of the judges. He sat next to her, smoking nervously as she chatted, and eventually he murmured: 'I don't talk much, Teresa.' Her reply? 'Don't worry, Bobby, I'll talk for both of us.' And I'm sure she did!

Bobby Charlton looked to have the making of true greatness when he broke through in 1956 – let's face it, he must have been pretty extraordinary to get Billy Whelan out of the team – and he fulfilled that potential to the letter.

Finally I must turn to the goalkeepers, a breed apart. The man between our posts as the Babes moved towards maturity, lifting two League Championships and blazing a trail into Europe in the process, was Ray Wood. He arrived in Manchester in December 1949, some three months before me, having signed from Darlington as a green but immensely promising teenager. After being pitched straight into senior action against Newcastle, during an injury crisis, Ray returned to the reserves to hone his craft, learning plenty from the likes of Jack Crompton and Reg Allen and proving such an apt pupil that by 1954 he had won a handful of England caps. A capable all-round performer, Woodie was especially quick on his feet, a legacy from youthful days as a professional sprinter in the pit villages near his home. That speed proved invaluable to his defenders, and I recall vividly several occasions when he left his line like lightning to spare our blushes by gathering risky back-passes. Unquestionably Ray did a splendid job throughout the mid 1950s, right up until the 1957 FA Cup Final against Aston Villa in which he was injured controversially (more of that later).

To that point there had been no real talk of a replacement for Ray, who was only 26 at the time, no age for a goalkeeper, but Matt Busby was always looking to improve the side and he did that the following December by making Harry Gregg the world's costliest custodian. It sounds chicken-feed in these days of ridiculously inflated prices, but the fiery, red-haired Ulsterman was acquired for the princely sum of £23,500 from Second Division Doncaster Rovers, and critics reckoned Matt must have lost his marbles to pay so much for a goalkeeper! In fact, Harry was an absolute bargain, equalling the shot-stopping brilliance of Ray Wood but bringing an extra dimension to his work, that of commanding his penalty area. Harry would charge from his line to claim the ball no matter who or what was in his way. Every time a ball came across he believed it should be his, and sometimes it seemed that he handed out as many bruises to team-mates as to opponents, so vigorous were his forays. It didn't matter if it was the mighty Duncan Edwards or the greenest of rookies, they all had to make way when Harry Gregg left his line. Sadly his bravery cost him many an injury, which restricted him horribly later in his career, but not before he had been voted the top 'keeper in the 1958 World Cup, starring as Northern Ireland reached the quarter-finals. Because of what we were to go through together at Munich, I believe there has always been a certain bond between the two of us, and that continues to this day.

In addition to Ray and Harry, there was an athletic young Lancastrian name of David Gaskell, who was called on as a substitute for Woodie in the 1956 FA Charity Shield against Manchester City at Maine Road. He had bags of natural talent, which was was matched by his confidence and his courage, and at one point it seemed that he might make the position his own. But then he suffered a succession of injuries, perhaps a little nervousness crept in, and in the end David never became a long-term regular.

There were plenty of other players pushing for a place in the late 1950s, such men as wing-halves Wilf McGuinness and Freddie Goodwin, full-back Ian Greaves, centre-half Ronnie Cope, and forwards Colin Webster, Alex Dawson and Mark Pearson. They were all good footballers without being in the absolute top bracket at the time, although it should be said that Wilf made more than a century of appearances for United and won two England caps before his playing days were ended by a cruel injury, so we can never know exactly what he might have achieved given better fortune. As it was, he worked prodigiously hard hard and loved the club with every bit of his being. It should be said, too, that Mark and Alex were youngsters who might have developed further had they not been pushed into senior action rather too soon – albeit out of stark necessity – in the immediate aftermath of Munich.

Away from the game, these fellows loved a bit of fun, especially Wilf, who was – and remains, for that matter! – a silver-tongued devil, a boyishly light-hearted lad who relished a bit of banter and a practical joke. I have this abiding image of him taking his cartilage, which had been removed in a recent operation, on to the team bus in a bottle of spirit, and trying to revolt some of the wives by waving it under their noses. Colin could be a bit of a rascal, too, but there was no harm in him. Whatever, they were all Busby Babes, and they were all part of the most stimulating club scene imaginable.

# Five

# Cloak, dagger... and a title gong

**W**HEN I began life as a Red Devil, Matt Busby was a father figure to me. I looked up to him in everything, he gave me sound advice on football and he played a massive part in my development. It's fair to say, also, that he was overwhelmingly persuasive.

Matt was a soccer visionary who saw, as his first fine team grew old at the end of the 1940s, that the only viable future for Manchester United was with young footballers. But contrary to legend and popular perception, he did not have a monopoly on the idea. Other clubs were desperate to sign the finest rookie talent, too, but where Matt had the jump on his competitors was in his attention to detail. Where his rivals would send a scout to speak to an exceptional boy, and to his family, the United boss would take the trouble to call round himself. He was a wonderfully charming man, adept at the sweet talk, and there were few parents he could not convince. Undoubtedly his most spectacular conquest was that of Duncan Edwards, when he turned up on the boy's doorstep in the early hours of his 14th birthday. Duncan lived in Dudley, which was heartland territory of Wolverhampton Wanderers, and Molineux boss Stan Cullis had been equally as keen as his Old Trafford counterpart to sign the most sought-after schoolboy in the game; but it was Matt who made the personal effort and Matt who claimed the prize. A fascinating parallel can be drawn with Alex Ferguson snatching young Ryan Giggs from under the noses of Manchester City more than a third of a century later.

I was never in the star category and Matt did not need his silver tongue to induce me to join United, but soon after I had made my senior debut in 1952/53, he was using it to bend my ear, albeit with typical subtlety, on a regular basis. At the time I remained a part-time footballer, earning far more down the mine than I did from Manchester United, and I was loth to relinquish the security that represented while Matt, not unnaturally, desired my full attention. The fact was that, having risen to become an assistant under-manager at the colliery, I was pocketing £15 a week, which was a substantial wage for a young man at that time. In contrast, my early pay packets from the club contained £7 during the season, falling to £6 in the summer. As for prospects, I might have gone a long way with the Coal Board but, with the football authorities enforcing a maximum wage, I could see that Allenby Chilton, for example, a loyal and long-term servant of the club, was receiving a mere £17.

Having known lean times himself, back in his Lanarkshire youth, the boss appreciated my financial viewpoint, but nevertheless he wasted no opportunity to impress on me that, football-wise, both the team and myself would benefit if I turned professional. Looking back now, I suppose it seems scarcely credible that I was playing at the top club level, yet I was training with my team-mates only twice a week. For all that, it was not until I had nearly two seasons of regular First Division appearances under my belt, and had satisfied myself that I had a long-term future in the game, that I capitulated to his constant pressure. A turning point in my mental process was selection for what proved to be my only full England cap, against Northern Ireland in Belfast in October 1954. I reasoned that if I were good enough to play for my country, then I need have no fears about slipping out of football.

By modern standards, my experiences on the day of that international match must seem bizarre. Though suffering from a streaming cold, I had completed a full shift down the mine in the morning before joining the England team at 2.30 pm in Manchester and travelling to Ireland for the game, which was played some 24 hours later. Then it was straight back home in time to disappear down the shaft again! I imagine that whoever is chosen to replace Steve McClaren as England boss would not be too enamoured of such antics in 2008! Even in 1954 it was anything but ideal, though I believe I acquitted myself well enough at right-back in subduing a rumbustious attacker name of Peter McParland, who was to feature prominently in the United story several years down the line. It helped that I was operating alongside my Old Trafford full-back partner, Roger Byrne, and in front of United 'keeper Ray Wood. They put me at my ease, and both England boss Walter Winterbottom and the skipper, Billy Wright, seemed happy with my performance. Yet I was never picked again, which still rankles with me all these years later. True, I was surprised to be selected in the first place, having played only some 20 senior games, and I wasn't really ready for the international arena, but what is the point in picking a 22-year-old, giving him one game in which he does reasonably well, and then discarding him for good? I was replaced briefly by 29-year-old Ron Staniforth of Huddersfield Town, before the selection committee granted similarly fleeting stints to Manchester City's Jimmy Meadows and Peter Sillett of Chelsea. After that, admittedly, poor Jeff Hall of Birmingham City was given a decent run, which was ended tragically by his death of polio. The subsequent inheritors of the number-two shirt were Don Howe (West Bromwich Albion) and Jimmy Armfield (Blackpool), by which time I was playing at centre-half, which I consider to be my best position. Alas, England never gave me an opportunity in that role, so my international career – which also included a couple of outings for the Football League at around that time – was over almost as soon as it had begun.

Back on the club scene, I had bedded into the first team during 1953/54, displacing Tommy McNulty at right-back in September and thereafter missing only one game, through injury, for the remainder of the campaign. We were still a side in transition, with more and more Babes being added, but although we never looked likely to equal the Championship achievement of 1951/52, I felt we were attaining more consistency than in 1952/53, when we had been ninth. In the circumstances a fourth-place finish, nine points behind top club Wolves, was tolerably satisfactory and I registered one personal milestone by scoring my first senior goal. To be honest, though, my winner in a 2-1 victory at Newcastle was a bit of a fluke. There was a gale blowing and when I took possession from Johnny Berry, some ten yards inside my own half, I aimed for the head of Tommy Taylor, who was sprinting towards the Magpies' far post. But the wind caught the ball and it sailed over poor Ronnie Simpson and hit the net without touching the ground. If that happened today, I'd be hailed as a superstar, another Beckham, but unlike David, who flighted his famous effort at Wimbledon so perfectly, there was no way I could claim a precision delivery.

A less welcome 'first' for me that term was what turned out to be the only bona fide caution of my career (later I was booked again, but that was rubbed out on appeal). It happened in November at Ninian Park, where we won 6-1 but I allowed Cardiff City's Welsh international left-winger George Edwards to rub me up the wrong way. Despite our dominance, he insisted on taking the mickey out of me, and eventually I snapped, hitting him with a crazy tackle which lifted him over the fence and into the crowd. It was stupid of me and I was lucky to get away with a mere booking – these days, undoubtedly, I would have been red-carded – and afterwards Matt Busby had a sharp word with me. He stressed that if I couldn't control myself, then I was no use to the team, and I heeded that lesson. That didn't mean that I was any less physical, I was always a hard player, but I never let the red mist descend again and stayed essentially within the rules. In fact, Mark Jones, who was as tough as they came but a lovely character, used to say to me: 'I wish I could be like you, Bill, and kick them in cold blood!'

Come 1954/55 we continued to develop, playing with enormous

verve on occasions, and it seemed only a matter of time before we hit the top, but still we could manage no better than fifth place. However, it all came right in 1955/56, when the likes of Duncan, Tommy and the rest had all settled in, meshing so brilliantly that we romped to the title, finishing 11 points clear of runners-up Blackpool. That term proved a watershed to me, not just because of my first Championship medal, but also because Matt Busby had finally persuaded me to become a full-time footballer. He promised me that if I did so I would avoid National Service; perhaps he thought he could pull a few strings behind the scenes. On this occasion, though, it appears that his eloquence proved unavailing because, just two weeks after taking the professional plunge, I was called up by the Army. I wasn't happy because he had managed to get Mark Jones out of the draft on the pretext of flat feet, which seemed ridiculous to me, and David Pegg escaped because he walked in his sleep! I was convinced that I would be excused because Teresa, my wife of five months, was suffering from TB and I had to look after her while pursuing my career. I couldn't credit that Teresa's serious condition was not considered as important as Mark's feet and David's night-time perambulations. When I went for my medical I laid heavy emphasis on my wife's plight, and told the doctors that I had symptoms of the disease, too. That was a load of nonsense, of course, but I was willing to try anything to avoid the Army. One fellow put me on a machine and told me to breathe deeply, then he called in two colleagues and said: 'Bloody hell, look at this.' My heart sank. I thought he'd discovered that I was suffering from something serious, but the next minute he admitted that he'd merely sent for some fellow medics to view the fantastic expansion of my lungs! So there was nothing for it but to join up, and Duncan Edwards and I were ordered to report to a station in Piccadilly, Manchester, where there was momentary hope of a reprieve because of a rail strike. Unfortunately for us a truck ride was soon organised; Duncan was bound for Woolwich Barracks and I was off to Blandford Forum in Dorset for ten weeks of initial training.

After all Matt's assurances, conscription came as a bombshell and, as a result, the Foulkes household faced financial turmoil and a certain amount of hardship. From having two salaries, a substantial one from the Coal Board and my United wages, suddenly I was guaranteed no more than the weekly fifteen shillings and six old pence that I would receive from the Army. The club, it seemed, would pay me only for the games in which I played. Even if Matt picked me, which he did for most of the season, still it was up to me to get to the games, from wherever in the country I happened to be stationed – and that could prove horrendously difficult. As a result of this drastic reduction in our resources, poor Teresa had to go out to work, even though she was ill. It was an outrageous situation, but we had to make the best of it.

On being drafted into the Royal Army Service Corps I was dispatched to Aldershot as a driver, and when I explained my position to a sympathetic commanding officer, he gave me some welcome – and strictly unofficial – advice on how to manage my time. It seemed that he couldn't allot me a pass out of the barracks for every game, every week, so my appearance record in what would prove a momentous season for Manchester United would be up to me. In essence, he told me to invest in a snazzy trilby, a voluminous overcoat and a smart briefcase, and to give the Military Police as wide a berth as possible. Because I was a little older than most new soldiers, having had my call-up deferred during my previous occupation as a mineworker, he thought I might get away with going AWOL. And I did, playing in 27 League and FA Cup games, for many of which I turned up in disguise!

I began as I meant to continue on the first day of the season. We were away to Birmingham City and Matt had told me that if I made it to St Andrews then I would play, though perhaps he didn't really expect me to keep the date. I was square-bashing in Blandford at the time and I informed my platoon sergeant (who was a Celtic supporter) that I was going over the top because I had to play for United. His response was: 'No passes, pal' but I declared that I was going anyway, so he said I must take the consequences. Whatever happened, it was nothing to do with him. At that time I hadn't even sorted out my disguise, but luck was with me. I arrived safely at St Andrews and was standing outside the main gate when United's coach rolled up. As soon as Matt caught sight of me he held his head in his hands; he knew he had made an agreement and now he would have to keep it. He told me to go into the dressing room and I could see he was embarrassed, obviously having told someone else, probably Ian Greaves, that he would be playing. But he was as good as his word and I turned out in an exciting 2-2 draw in which Dennis Viollet scored both our goals.

I suppose I sailed pretty close to the wind, at times, with my cloak-and-dagger travelling arrangements. At one point I knew I was to move from Blandford to Buller Barracks at Aldershot, so after playing for United I skipped returning to camp and went home with the team, then visited Teresa before going back to Dorset. I went straight to the guardroom to face it out and was greeted by: 'Are you Driver Foulkes? F****** get outside. There's a guy in a car who's been waiting for you for 24 hours.' I wondered what was in store, but he took me to Buller Barracks, where I was to remain for the rest of my Army career. I lived a protected existence there, billeted in a civilian hut just off the canteen, with no inspections and few duties. That had been arranged by the CO, who enjoyed the kudos which came his way from the Army football team, of which I was captain. I was a lucky man and I knew it.

Of course, even though a blind eye was being turned at my base, that didn't alter the strain I was under constantly because of my nerve-shredding journeys, and also there was the worry that someone in authority might react to seeing my name mentioned regularly in newspaper reports of United's matches. Somehow I led a charmed life because I was never rumbled, though frequently I saw other people being apprehended by military police at railway stations. Towards the end of my service, United started flying me to games, which removed a lot of the pressure, but back in January 1956 I was so stressed amd stretched that it affected my form. Matt recognised this and duly I received a call from our coach, the endlessly supportive Bert Whalley, to tell me that I wouldn't be needed for the next match. Ian Greaves stepped in and kept his place for the rest of the season, playing extremely well and deserving his title medal. But I had already played 26 games, so I qualified for one, too, and I felt no sense that I was losing out long term. It was up to me and I was utterly determined to win back my place.

As for the Championship-winning campaign itself, it was the logical culmination of the steady improvement we had been achieving since the Babes had begun replacing the grand old 48-ers. We began slowly, with only three wins in the first eight matches, leaving Blackpool, Preston, Wolves and Charlton to make the early pace. But by December United's intermittent flair was buttressed by increased consistency and resounding victories at West Bromwich (4-1) on Christmas Eve and at home to Charlton (5-1) on Boxing Day – Dennis Viollet plundered five goals over the two games – lifted us four points clear. Psychologically, perhaps, we relaxed a little when we faced Charlton at the Valley on December 27, losing 3-0 in our third match in four days over the holiday period – and just as an aside, what on earth would today's highly-paid stars make of such a schedule? However, with that setback out of our collective system, we embarked on a run which saw us defeated only once more all season and in the end we topped the table by an emphatic 11 points. It was a magnificent effort by a line-up which most frequently read: Wood; Foulkes, Byrne; Colman, Jones, Edwards; Berry, Blanchflower, Taylor, Viollet, Pegg. Also there were medals for Jeff Whitefoot, who had occupied the right-half slot until the emergence of Eddie; for Liam Whelan and John Doherty, who had vied with Jackie Blanchflower at inside-right and each enjoyed a lengthy spell in possession; for utility forward Colin Webster; and for Ian Greaves who, as mentioned, took over from me towards the end. It was a hugely satisfying achievement but – and this was crucial – it felt very much more like a beginning than an end in itself.

Having come together, the Busby Babes felt there was no limit to what they could attain.

Meanwhile there was football in the Army, too, and it was of a high standard. I turned out for my battalion in the Hampshire Senior League and we won the Hampshire Cup, after my CO had encouraged me to grab professional players from different camps all over the country. Sadly we lost the Army Cup Final, thanks to a late rule change which meant we could field only three professionals instead of eight. I had worked very hard on that team and felt cheated, but at full Army level it was extremely satisfying to skipper a star-studded line-up which included the likes of Duncan Edwards and Bobby Charlton from United, Maurice Setters (then West Bromwich Albion, later United), Charlie Hurley (Sunderland), Peter Swan (Sheffield Wednesday), Jimmy Armfield (Blackpool), Graham Shaw (Sheffield United), Dave Dunmore and Cliff Jones (Tottenham). We played teams from all over Europe, which offered invaluable experience for subsequent continental excursions with United, a positive aspect of National Service of which I'm certain Matt Busby was acutely aware.

# Six

# Trailblazing

I N THE early autumn of 1956 Manchester United were poised on the threshold of the most challenging, absorbing, downright exhilarating season any British club had ever known to that point. We were the reigning English champions, our squad was deep enough to cover practically any eventuality and included at least four or five world-class performers, we were guided by the wisest of all managers … no wonder we were confident of being the first club to lift the coveted League and FA Cup double during the 20th century. In addition, and even more thrillingly, we were about to blaze a trail for English clubs in Europe, which represented a giant leap into the unknown.

Entry into the European Cup brought a whole new dimension to our lives and we were overjoyed to be the pioneers. When the competition had been launched in 1955, Chelsea, as champions, had been invited to take part but had not entered on the advice of our hidebound football authorities, who appeared to believe that involvement in Europe would prove somehow detrimental to the domestic game. Talk about closed minds! Exactly the opposite was true. The European Cup offered new horizons, fresh standards by which to measure our own stature, and Matt Busby realised that it represented the future.

When Chelsea had spurned the invitation, most football followers in the North of England were totally disgusted, viewing the Stamford

Bridge club's decision as pathetically weak-kneed and unimaginative. When it came to United's turn, Matt stood up to the authorities, refusing to compromise his principles – in exactly the same way as he had confronted the United board when there had been attempts to interfere with his managerial sovereignty soon after he took over at Old Trafford. We were proud of him for being so strong and so far-sighted, and as a result he became even more of an icon to fans and footballers alike. All the players were desperately keen to begin the European adventure. We had a burning desire to face different types of opponents in foreign lands, and to experience air travel. It conjured up a whole new world and we were transfixed by the possibilities, by the sheer romance of it all. The prospect caught the imagination of the crowds, too, and attendances soared accordingly. With all this going on, and despite the inconvenient circumstance that I was embarking on my second year of National Service, I decided that there was no way I was going to be left out of the side. So I dedicated myself to regaining my place from Ian Greaves, working like a madman to become fitter than ever before, and it paid off. When the season began, I was back in possession of Manchester United's number-two shirt.

We began our epic continental journey with a 2-0 triumph over Anderlecht in Belgium, where goals by Dennis Viollet and Tommy Taylor set the seal on a classy display, but it was the return in Manchester – played at Maine Road because the Old Trafford floodlights were not ready – which really made the European footballing fraternity sit up and take notice. That night we trounced the Belgians 10-0 with as irresistible an exhibition of attacking football as I have ever witnessed. This time Dennis notched four, Tommy grabbed a hat-trick, there were two for Billy Whelan and one for Johnny Berry, but the star man on the night was the only forward not to register, David Pegg. He created at least four of the goals, and we tried like hell to ensure that his name appeared on the scoresheet, but somehow he didn't manage it. He was given the ball in splendid positions several times, but he seemed reluctant to shoot, instead flicking passes to team-mates who continued to pile up the strikes. No matter, Manchester United had laid down a significant marker against a good team – despite a few sneers in the southern press about the quality of the opposition, Anderlecht played to a genuinely high standard – and we could march into the next round without any vestige of an inferiority complex.

There we met Borussia Dortmund and the two sides served up a classic confrontation between youthful exuberance and wily experience, with the Babes winning through by the narrowest of margins. At Maine Road we surged into a three-goal lead, but then were pegged back to 3-2 at the death and it needed a spirited rearguard action to see us through in the replay on the Ruhr. Borussia attacked unceasingly that night and Ray Wood played magnificently to keep a clean sheet as we held on for a goalless draw.

That saw us through to the quarter-finals against Athletic Bilbao, and I could hardly wait for the flight to Spain for the first leg. I hate flying now, for obvious reasons I suppose, but in those days I loved it. Nothing bothered me; the plane could have flown upside down for all I cared. I could have gone for a ride on a kite and enjoyed it. But, back in January 1957, some of the lads had serious misgivings as they climbed aboard our rather basic chartered Dakota, which started pitching up and down like a yo-yo soon after take-off. Certainly Mark Jones and Billy Whelan were ill throughout the trip and couldn't wait for it to end. I was sat at the front, cramped up behind a bulkhead unable to get comfortable, so I decided to put my feet up and pass the time by sleeping. The next thing I remember is an unholy commotion, with everyone complaining that they were freezing. A steward declared that the heating was on as high as it would go, but still the temperature was icy, especially at the back of the aircraft where our 74-year-old chairman, Harold Hardman, was shivering but sticking it manfully, without a murmur.

All at once I realised what had happened. I had been resting my feet on the lever which controlled the heating system, and by forcing it down I had shut off all warmth, causing the entire party almost to freeze to death. Poor Mr Hardman, who had turned blue with the cold, suffered hypothermia and a mild stroke, having to be rushed to hospital in Spain. He was unable to attend the match and missed the plane home, and it was all because of me. Of course, it had been wholly unintentional but I felt terrible about the situation, my state of mind hardly helped by the stick I received from my team-mates, who gave me the ironic nickname of PB – Popular Bill!

Still there were more problems to endure. After experiencing terrible winter weather all the way south, I consoled myself that at least it would be warm and sunny when we reached Bilbao. But all too soon I discovered that my childlike impression of Spain, based wholly on holiday posters at railway stations, was chronically misleading. To start with the cloud was so thick that our pilot took ages to even find the airport – he had us glueing our noses to the windows in search of a runway – and when we did touch down we disembarked to find slush and filth everywhere. There followed an uncomfortable, lurching ride in a rickety old coach through curtains of almost horizontal sleet along a heavily rutted road, beside which people were living like animals in shacks that were no better than slums. Next came difficulties with our food at the hotel, where the people were very friendly but insisted on serving ham and eggs in some sort of jelly, with luke-warm tea. Fortunately our club secretary Walter Crickmer, who was destined to lose his life at Munich, was a resourceful fellow and he proceeded to dispense lessons in English cooking to the kitchen staff, who mercifully proved to be quick learners.

The match didn't go according to plan, either. The pitch was little better than a swamp, consisting of snow and mud in equal measure, and it became ever more treacherous as rain continued to pelt down. Still we played well – Eddie Colman was particularly outstanding in midfield, seeming to skate over the slimy surface – but although we enjoyed far more of the game than Bilbao, they took their chances on the break and near the end we were 5-2 down. Then came Billy Whelan's wonder-goal, when he dribbled the leaden ball past a posse of defenders before beating the 'keeper with a thunderbolt, and we finished two adrift.

Afterwards all we wanted to do was to escape back to Manchester as quickly as possible, but leaving the Basque country was not going to be straightforward. On returning to the airport we found that our plane had been left out in a snowstorm and now was coated in slushy snow, while there was thick ice on the runway. Of course, we couldn't know it at the time but this scene represented a chilling glimpse of what awaited at Munich just over a year later. We were dismayed by the prospect of delay, especially as several of the lads had picked up stomach ailments at the hotel, and there would have been a hell of a row with the English authorities if we got back to England too late to fulfil our League fixture on the Saturday. So we asked the crew what we could do to help and they told us we could sweep the snow and slush from the aircraft. Accordingly a few of us seized brushes and set to work, while Billy Whelan's camera recorded the bizarre scene for posterity. We all had a laugh about it at the time, but in the light of the subsequent tragedy the incident takes on a positively macabre aspect.

Even with the wings and fuselage swept we were anything but home and dry. After getting off the ground in Bilbao we were tossed all over the shop by a ferocious storm, then were subjected to a terrifyingly bumpy landing on the clifftop runway at Jersey, where we touched down to refuel. Mark Jones, David Pegg, Geoff Bent and one or two others were turning green by then, though I was still not turning a hair. At that point I was still in love with flying and it was all part of the general excitement. Since Munich it has been a different story, and frequently I have been scared almost out of my wits when I have encountered even relatively mild turbulence.

Three weeks later we met Bilbao in the return leg at Maine Road, which turned out to be a classic, certainly the most thrilling game I had ever played in to that point. Faced with a two-goal deficit, and howled on by 65,000 fans, we tore into the Spaniards from the first whistle, and it was no more than we deserved when Dennis Viollet put us in front on the night shortly before the interval. Of course, that racheted up the tension even more and the noise rose to a permanent crescendo – hell, there must have been a few heart attacks on the terraces! – as we resumed the assault. Dennis was on fire and he had the ball in the net twice within a few minutes, but both efforts were disallowed controversially. Tommy was having a colossal dual with the Spanish centre-half, Jesus Garay, who must have been about the best stopper in the world in his day. The Bilbao man must have thought he had the measure of our centre-forward, but Tommy never gave up even as time was ticking away. At last, with about 18 minutes left and United still trailing on aggregate by one goal, he slipped away from his marker only to hit the Spaniards' post. Still we poured forward, though, still believing that we could do it, and suddenly we were level when Eddie Colman slipped a quick free-kick to Tommy, who gave goalkeeper Carmelo no chance. That made it 5-5 overall and now it was like the Charge of the Light Brigade as we went for the winner. The crowd was hysterical, the loudest I had ever experienced, and really there could be only one outcome. Sure enough, with just six minutes left, Tommy – whose phenomenal exertions that night would have brought a lesser man to his knees – somehow dredged up the energy to go past two defenders on the right wing before crossing to Johnny Berry, with whom he had swapped positions and who had drifted free of his attendants in the middle. The little fella hit the ball sweet and low, and it almost broke the back of the net. The place erupted, I thought we would be blasted off the pitch by the sheer force of all that celebration. Now we were 3-0 up in the game, 6-5 in the tie, but still it was not over as I almost found out to my cost with about a minute to go. In attempting to play out time I dispatched a pass-back to Ray Wood from near the right touchline and my heart froze as it stuck in the mud near the edge of the box. The Bilbao centre-forward seemed odds-on to score but Ray left his line like a cheetah and won the race for the ball. His speed had saved my bacon and ensured that Manchester United had reached the last four of the European Cup at the first attempt. At the end I felt both elation and relief, but also I spared a thought for Jesus Garay, who had performed so nobly that he didn't deserve to be on the losing side. Tommy Taylor had one of his best games for us, but Garay climbed with him every time, battling every inch of the way. He wasn't the best-known centre-half in Europe, but I don't know that I ever saw a more accomplished one.

We had passed a searching examination with flying colours, but our next test was to be even more demanding. In the semi-finals we drew Real Madrid, holders of the trophy and, by common consent, the finest team in the world. After our ordeal in Bilbao, I was faintly apprehensive about an immediate return to 'sunny' Spain, but this time it lived up to all my previous expectations. Apart from a totally different weather experience, this time our charter flight was better organised, and we were feted like pop stars from the moment we touched down in Madrid. We were given a tumultuous reception, with about a hundred photographers lying in wait at the airport, and duly we hammed it up for them, borrowing Matt's trilby hat for the purpose. The hotel, the food, the shopping, it was all first-class, and it felt like we had stepped into a whole new world after the dreary surroundings in Bilbao. Football-wise, it might have been expected that the manager would prepare us for the quantum leap in quality with which we were to be confronted by compiling extensive dossiers on Real's star players and their tactics, but nothing could have been further from the truth. When we ran out at the Bernabeu, engulfed by a rolling wall of sound generated by some 135,000 fanatical supporters, we knew next to nothing about our illustrious opponents. Of course, we knew they were a magnificent side, but Matt had not burdened us with any details. Perhaps he had decided that the less we knew the better!

At the hub of everything for Real Madrid was the incomparable Argentinian, Alfredo di Stefano. He played with a number nine on his back, but in a deep-lying position from which he could dictate proceedings. In England we were used to playing at one speed and that was 100 mph. But he would change the pace constantly, slowing to a walk, then delivering a sudden clever pass that would enable the left-winger, Francisco Gento, to use his explosive pace. Then there was big Hector Rial, a countryman of di Stefano's and a brilliant inside-forward who specialised in beautiful passes into space behind defenders. That suited Gento perfectly, and as right-back I was in direct opposition to him. It was not an easy ride against 'El Motor-Bike', as they called him. Apart from his outlandish pace, he had fantastic control and a knack of stopping the ball dead just before it went out of play. For much of the time there was little I could do except try to block the cross, or try to cover if he did deliver the ball into the centre. It's fair to say I was stretched, but after the game Matt Busby said that no full-back in England could have played him better, so I was pretty pleased with that. In fact, although we lost 3-1, our whole defence was superb and in the words of our trainer, Tom Curry, we deserved gold medals as big as frying pans. Though we managed to worry Real on the break, especially through the indomitable Tommy Taylor, we were on the back foot for a lot of the time. That said, we held our nerve to keep the scoresheet blank at the interval, but couldn't repeat the performance in the second half, when they scored three against Tommy's lone reply. Still, we were not outclassed, and had a couple of decent penalty appeals turned down, especially one when Johnny Berry was flattened in the acting of shooting into the net. For all their artistry, Real were a very physical side, with even the stars capable of handing out punishment, as Jackie Blanchflower discovered in excruciatingly painful circumstances. After breaking up an attack with typical composure, our Irish centre-half pushed the ball through di Stefano's legs and made to sidestep the great man before moving forward. But Alfredo was too cute for that; there was no way he was going to be nutmegged and the next moment, bang, our man was on the floor. I came running up, ready to step in if there was a problem, and Jackie muttered through gritted teeth: 'Have a word with him, Foulkesy!' I was in control of myself, and I didn't intend for the situation to get out of hand, but I thought a point needed to be made so I scowled menacingly at the Argentinian as though there was murder on my mind. He responded with an uncertain glance followed by a placatory smile and what I took to be an apology: 'Okay Foulk-ez' he said, spreading his hands as if in admission of guilt. Since that day I have met him many times, and always he recalls the incident with a laugh. I must have made an impression.

At 3-1 down after the first leg, we remained firmly in contention so the return at Old Trafford – where we were due to play our first match under our new floodlights – was a truly momentous occasion. Unfortunately we were undone by our understandable inexperience in European competition, attacking like demons from the off instead of taking a more measured approach. That played into the hands of Real, who soaked up the pressure before countering to devastating effect with goals from Kopa and Mateos. Even so, they never really came to terms with the aerial power of Tommy Taylor and if he had received even a smidgin of protection from the referee, we might have rattled them. There were times when Madrid defenders were literally hanging on to Tommy's shirt to keep him on the ground, and they got away with it. Still we never gave up, and goals from Taylor and the young Bobby Charlton crowned a memorable struggle, and earned an honourable draw on the night. Overall I wouldn't deny that the best team won, but we had learned a lot which we took with us into the next phase of our European development. As for Real Madrid, it had been a privilege to play them. They had so many world-class performers, such men as Raymond Kopa of the silky skills, pinpoint cross and lethal finish; Francisco Gento, who was so blindingly quick and impossibly elusive; Hector Rial, who was like a professor with his slide-rule passing; and, above all, the fabulous Alfredo, whom I would choose as the greatest all-round footballer I have ever seen; and, yes, that includes Pele. It had been an exhilarating adventure and, so we all believed, the first of many.

Back on the domestic front, events had been running smoothly. With the competition for places at Old Trafford as white-hot as ever, the team was improving all the time and Matt Busby believed he was getting closer and closer to the realisation of his footballing vision. Though I was still in the Army, I hardly missed a match, having got the complicated travel arrangements down to a fine art, but I was always aware that my standard could not slip even marginally, such was the exceptional quality of our reserves. We began with a 2-2 draw at home to Birmingham before launching on a free-scoring winning streak, not losing until we nosedived 5-2 at home to Everton in late October. The side was basically the same as in 1955/56 but with the occasional addition of Bobby Charlton, who made a dramatic senior entrance with two goals at home to Charlton Athletic, and I wasn't surprised when we romped away with a second successive Championship, which we had wrapped up by Easter.

Yet for all our League joy, and our swashbuckling progress in Europe, there had been one area in which we had under-achieved during the mid 1950s, and that was the FA Cup. In 1953/54 we had perished in the third round at Burnley, then a season later Manchester City saw us off at Maine Road in the fourth – incidentally just a couple of days after Teresa and I got married – before United reached new knockout depths, being thrashed 4-0 by Bristol Rovers in 1955/56. That was a shattering experience for a side sitting proudly on top of the First Division, and the unpalatable truth was that the second-flight Pirates thoroughly deserved their comprehensive victory that day at Eastville. People looked for excuses, but really there weren't any. Certainly there was no question of United fielding a below-strength side in the FA Cup, as they have done occasionally in the modern era. True we were without Duncan Edwards and Billy Whelan through injury, but we had top-notch replacements in Jeff Whitefoot and John Doherty, and Rovers could declare truthfully that they had whipped the pre-Munich Busby Babes. Their two main strikers, Alfie Biggs and Geoff Bradford, gave us the run-around, and it wasn't a case of being hustled out of our stride. The pair of them could really play football and we hadn't expected anything like them. True the pitch was heavy and the atmosphere was extremely partisan – with a crowd of more than 35,000 fans, quite a few of whom seemed to be hanging from the rafters – but we should have been able to cope with that. Instead we disintegrated, and we got what we deserved. I guess we must have been victims of over-confidence and Matt was not happy. On the train trip down from Manchester we had played cards and a few players, including myself, had lost some wages. In my case it was £8, pretty well the whole contents of one of my earlier paypackets as a professional. On the way back the school started again and that was enough for our manager, who snatched up the cards and the money and threw them out of the window. No one so much as murmured. We knew we had let ourselves and the club down, and the Boss was entitled to be upset. I doubt if the thought of crossing him even entered anyone's head. That pretty well finished me with cards, and on reflection I think Matt was right. My view at the time was that I had chosen to play and it was no one's fault but my own that I had lost a week's wages. However, such a situation could easily cause resentment between players, which could prove disastrous for team spirit. Matt was a bit of a gambler himself – he liked the horses – and he understood how disastrous the effects of losing could be. The same thing happened a few years later after a defeat at Leicester, with cards and cash being swept out of a train window. By that time, though, I had enough sense not to be involved.

To return to the FA Cup, with such a background of recent under-achievement in the oldest of all professional football competitions, we were determined to do rather better in 1956/57 – and so we did, though it felt that every step of the way was punctuated by high drama, and the eventual outcome was hardly what we had in mind. Our FA Cup trail began at Hartlepools United, who were then riding high in the old Third Division North, and what a fright they gave us! We cruised into a three-goal lead at the Victoria Ground, but were given a sharp reminder of previous frailties when our hosts fought back spiritedly to level pegging, and it must have been mortifying for them when Billy Whelan spoiled their celebrations with a late winner. Next came a 5-0 win at Wrexham which was not as comfortable as it sounds, with the Welshmen pushing us extremely hard; then we squeezed past Everton by the only goal of a tight tie at Old Trafford before receiving another shock at the hands of so-called minnows in the quarter-finals. This time we were facing Bournemouth at Dean Court, and should have known what to expect because they had already toppled Wolves and Spurs during an eventful passage to the last eight. Pretty soon it looked as if Manchester United would become the Cherries' latest scalp as they took an interval lead, but eventually our blushes were spared thanks to a couple of second-half strikes from Johnny Berry. The little winger was on the mark again at the semi-final stage, putting us in front against his former employers, Birmingham City, at Hillsborough, and another goal from Bobby Charlton cemented our place at Wembley.

Now excitement reached fever pitch because, with the League already in our pockets, we were runaway favourites to become the first club to lift the League and FA Cup double during the 20th century. There had been a few near misses in recent years, but no one had quite managed it and a bit of a myth had grown up around it. Approaching the final against Aston Villa, we were confident, but certainly not complacent. Villa had earned their berth at Wembley the hard way, battling through replays against Luton in the third round, Burnley in the quarter-final and West Bromwich Albion in the semi-final, and they were not running out beneath the twin towers merely to be cannon fodder for United. True, we were smarting from our European Cup exit to Real Madrid only nine days earlier, but if anything that had sharpened our resolve not to be beaten again. Dennis Viollet was missing with a groin injury, but his deputy, Bobby Charlton, hardly weakened our attack, so the scene appeared to be set for the ultimate achievement in English club football.

But then fate took the cruellest of hands. Some six minutes into the action Ray Wood gathered a routine header from Peter McParland, then took a step forward with the ball safely in his arms as Villa's ultra-combative Irish left-winger hurtled towards him. In the instant that I had to think about it, I assumed that he would veer aside at the last moment, but he charged on and smashed into Ray at full throttle.

I could hardly believe my eyes because, to me, it was a deliberate head butt. McParland just hammered in and put his head straight into Ray's cheekbone, which was shattered by the impact. The point was that Ray had taken possession of the ball already, so it was no longer there to be challenged for. It was the clearest of fouls, and today McParland would have been sent off instantly. Had he been dismissed, it would have been ten men against ten – don't forget that in those days there were no substitutes, so we could not replace Woodie – and we would have had a fighting chance, even without a specialist goalkeeper. Instead, we had to reshuffle the team and Jackie Blanchflower went between the posts, with Duncan Edwards moving to centre-half and Billy Whelan dropping back to left-half. Then, irony of ironies, McParland went on to be the match-winner, scoring two goals in the space of six minutes midway through the second half. And as if that wasn't bad enough, he showed not a scrap of remorse for what he had done, claiming afterwards that it had been an honest accident when all the evidence suggested that he had clattered Ray in cold blood. Jackie, who was always a versatile player, handled himself superbly in goal and made some smashing saves, but he was helpless for McParland's goals. Still, overrun though we were, we pushed Villa back towards the end and Tommy gave us hope with a headed goal in the 83rd minute. That was the signal for the courageous Wood, who had returned to the action towards the end of the first half but only as a passenger on the wing, to risk further serious injury by going back in goal, and we threw everything at Villa in the dying minutes. Billy Whelan had the ball in the net but it was disallowed for offside and there were several more near misses but in the end our dream died. Even in such unfortunate circumstances, it had been a pulsating match, with both sides playing plenty of good football, and normally I'd be content to say 'well done' to the victors, no matter how disappointed I felt personally. But the Ray Wood episode was unsavoury, it left a bitter taste in the mouth, and we departed Wembley feeling we had been both unlucky and unfairly treated. Still, we could hold our heads high. We had suffered injustice but we had not retaliated by attempting to take physical revenge, instead just getting on with the job. As we made our sad way home, we were consoled by the confident prediction of our skipper, Roger Byrne, that Manchester United would return to Wembley in a year's time. He was right, of course, but poor Roger was not to be leading us and many of his team-mates would be missing, too, having been overtaken by tragedy at Munich.

For the time being, though, there were no such clouds on the Red Devils' horizons as we kicked off the 1957/58 campaign hotly tipped to complete a hat-trick of League titles. I felt wonderful. I had finished my National Service, and I was playing for the best team in the country which showed every sign of scaling multiple new peaks. Nothing could have been better. At first everything went according to plan as we scored 22 goals in our first six games and soared to the top of the table. At that point the pundits were freely predicting an unheard-of treble of League, FA Cup and European Cup, and while we were not thinking in those terms, certainly the spirit in the Old Trafford camp could hardly have been more buoyant. But suddenly, for no apparent reason, the script started to go alarmingly awry. We were hammered at Bolton, then lost to Blackpool, Wolves, Portsmouth and West Bromwich Albion all in the space of six weeks. Matt didn't panic, but he reacted decisively, changing half the team about midway through the season. Wingers Berry and Pegg were dropped in favour of Morgans and Scanlon, Whelan made way for Charlton, Jones replaced Blanchflower and new signing Harry Gregg took over in goal from Ray Wood. There was no suggestion that those dropped would never have returned and they remained an integral part of the squad, though we shall never know for sure because Munich transformed the entire picture. Personally I'm certain that, but for the catastrophe, we would not have seen the last of Pegg, Whelan and Blanchflower, though Berry might have faced an uphill struggle because he was past 30. The one whose future seemed most dicy was Wood and sure enough, soon after surviving the crash, he left the club. Not that Matt wasn't happy with his squad – after buying Tommy Taylor in March 1953 there were no more major incoming transfers until Harry Gregg in December 1957 – it was just that he wasn't certain about the most effective combination. By today's standards, it is astonishing to contemplate a side remaining at the top of the English game for half a decade without making a single purchase.

Whatever, the changes Matt made in the early winter of 1957 had a salutary outcome. We embarked on a winning run and, even though we were a few points adrift of the League leaders by early February, I believe that we still had a great chance of retaining the Championship. Suddenly everything seemed right again, as our last two First Division performances before Munich illustrated graphically. A 7-2 home trouncing of Bolton, in which Bobby Charlton struck a hat-trick, was followed by one of the most enthralling contests of my career, a 5-4 victory over Arsenal in a Highbury mudbath. We attacked relentlessly throughout the first half, with Albert Scanlon in particular running the Gunners ragged – at that time, arguably, he was the best winger in the country – and by the interval we were comfortably in control through goals from Duncan Edwards, Bobby Charlton and Tommy Taylor. But perhaps complacency set in, and Arsenal punished us with three strikes in as many minutes, one from David Herd – later to excel as a Red Devil – and two from Jimmy Bloomfield. Now the Busby Babes demonstrated their true mettle, hauling themselves up by their bootstraps to regain the ascendancy through Dennis Viollet and Taylor, though Derek Tapscott pulled one back at the death. Had there been man-of-the-match awards in those days, I guess it would have gone to Albert, although Duncan gave a stupendous display, too. He was an absolute colossus, ploughing through the mud and winning pretty well every challenge, but also skimming his passes beautifully on such a squelchy surface. Above all it was a magnificent game of football, an out-and-out classic in which both teams had committed themselves wholeheartedly to attack, and one in which we had underlined our potential to recover lost ground in the title race. Of course, that never came to pass. What that north

London crowd of more than 63,000 supporters had witnessed was an epic epitaph to one of the great club sides, one which would never play again on English soil, and which would be torn apart by tragedy within a mere five days.

There was still time, though, for one more compelling display.

# Seven

# Calamity

THE MUNICH air crash is the most dramatic, and traumatic, single event in my life, and for a long time I tried to wipe it from my memory. But it would never go.

It came back to haunt me every time I climbed on to a plane, every time anyone mentioned the Busby Babes or the European Cup. Obviously these were subjects which kept on cropping up. Whenever there was a landmark anniversary of the disaster, I would be asked for interviews and I always helped to the best of my ability, but I cannot pretend that it wasn't painful. It still is, but I have learned to cope with the demons, put them in perspective, a process which I hope will be completed by the writing of this book.

All I recall of the outward flight to Belgrade, where we were to face the famous Red Star in a European Cup quarter-final second leg on 5 February 1958, was that I enjoyed the trip. I found it extremely pleasant. I didn't have the slightest worry about flying at that time. In fact, I relished each flight more than the last, a state of mind which was not destined to remain with me for much longer. On the way out we touched down at both Hamburg and Munich to refuel, and when we approached Belgrade we descended through low cloud and fog to find a carpet of snow on the ground.

My immediate impression of Belgrade was not a positive one. We had already derived some notion of life behind the Iron Curtain when we had visited Prague, the Czechoslovakian capital, where we had witnessed people queueing for food and discovered that getting anything decent to eat was an awful struggle. Belgrade was similarly depressing, although I've got to say that in Yugoslavia food did not seem to be quite so scarce. However, the overall atmosphere was one of poverty. The faces of the people on the streets seemed to be pinched with hardship. Clearly, life was anything but easy. Owing to our experiences in Prague, Manchester United had taken an enormous stock of tinned food, soup and fresh fruit this time. The club was determined that there would be no chance of us being on short rations. I can remember Albert Scanlon, who was my room-mate, waking me up at something like three o'clock in the morning to offer me an apple. Albert was a marvellous footballer and a smashing lad, but he could be a bit of a scatterbrain at times.

The weather was abominably cold and I remember people were skating near our hotel, which was a fabulously opulent place, run by the state seemingly only for the benefit of foreigners. Certainly, there was no sign of any local folks partaking of the luxury. It seemed as if they were putting on a show, but I hope the Yugoslavians did not delude themselves that they could kid us somehow that their people were living in similarly prosperous fashion under Communist rule. For all the oddness of that situation, though, it has to be admitted that the food, service and everything else at our hotel was absolutely first-class. We had no need of our carefully assembled hoard of provisions; in fact, we lacked for nothing at all.

As for the game, we were by far the better side, although it was clear that there was no shortage of Yugoslavians who did not share that opinion. It was never a rough or unruly encounter, but the home fans did not like what they considered to be our unduly tough tackling. For our part, we were less than enamoured with their typically continental tactics, which involved frequent petty infringements. We had won 2-1 in a tight game at Old Trafford and this second meeting finished 3-3, although we should have triumphed comfortably after taking a three-goal lead on a treacherous pitch which was partially covered with snow and ice.

We got off to a fantastic start when Dennis Viollet seized on a rebound and put us in front after only 90 seconds. About ten minutes later Bobby Charlton had the ball in the net, only to be flagged offside, but he was in fabulous form and was not to be denied on his first European trip. Before the interval he had scored two legitimate goals – including a superbly placed low 30-yarder – and so we went in with a 5-1 aggregate lead. That seemed to be that but Red Star, lifted by their beautifully artistic inside-forward Dragoslav Sekularac, were not giving up. Within two minutes of the restart they had reduced the arrears through Kostic, and then I was involved in a controversial incident which saw the gap diminish further. I went for the ball with Tasic, who appeared to fall over and I tumbled on top of him. The referee took the view – a wrong one in my opinion – that I had flattened my opponent and signalled for a penalty. Tasic himself converted from the spot, although Harry almost got his fingertips to the Yugoslav's shot and was unlucky not to save it.

After that the home supporters went crazy and Red Star, their confidence restored, began throwing everything at us. At one point Cokic seemed certain to equalise and a section of the crowd, straining forward to get a better view of the action, almost precipitated a tragedy. Dozens of people stumbled forwards and fell on top of one another, but as far as I know there were no serious injuries, though that was merely a matter of good fortune. Meanwhile the game raged on entertainingly and Kenny Morgans thumped an upright with a superbly struck drive, but a knife-edge finish was set up when Harry carried the ball outside his box and Kostic equalised with a free-kick which ricocheted into the net via Viollet's head. Now, with only three minutes left, we were just one goal to the good overall, but we managed to hold out without too much difficulty, thus reaching the last four of the European Cup for the second successive season.

Neither the Red Star players nor their supporters admired the way we got stuck into our tackles – even though we invariably went for the ball, usually coming away with it, too! – and after leaving the dressing room we were booed all the way back to our hotel. But then, to give them their due, they laid on a slap-up banquet in our honour. We were treated fantastically. There was plenty of sumptuous food, the finest wine flowed freely and there was exquisite music from some of Yugoslavia's leading violinists. The press boys were at the party, too. In those days we knew the lads from the newspapers almost as well as we knew each other and there was a camaraderie between us all. It was light years away from the virtual war footing which exists between players and sections of the press today.

After the feast, the people who worked in the British Embassy, who were obviously overjoyed by the successful English effort, took us to their homes and did their utmost to ply us with more drink. One of them presented me with a bottle of gin, which will crop up again later in the most unexpected manner. Next morning there were some very thick heads among the Manchester United party as we travelled to the airport by coach, many of us rather exhausted but extremely delighted with life.

One incident that sticks in my mind is some confusion about Johnny Berry. At one point it seemed the Yugoslavs were hell-bent on keeping our perky little right-winger in their country. There was a considerable, rather worrying delay while his visa and passport were sorted out to the satisfaction of the officials. Apparently it was found on the aircraft and eventually, after what seemed like an eternity, we were whisked off through something approaching a blizzard to Munich, where it was still snowing heavily as we landed for a refuelling stop.

Mrs Miklos, the wife of our courier – he was one of those destined to die in the crash – served us all with some much-needed coffee while the fuel was being pumped into our aircraft, and then we all trooped back on board again, just as bright and breezy as when we had left Yugoslavia. As we went up the steps, I asked the steward what time we could expect to land in Manchester. He consulted his watch and predicted that it should be around seven o'clock. At that time it must have been between three and four o'clock.

In the centre of the plane – a chartered twin-engined Elizabethan – David Pegg was sitting opposite me. We were both in window seats with Kenny Morgans alongside me and Albert Scanlon next to David. Matt Busby and Bert Whalley were sitting behind us. I was facing towards the tail of the plane and we had a card school going. Across the aisle there was a six-seater table where Roger Byrne, Billy Whelan, Ray Wood and Jackie Blanchflower were sat. Bobby Charlton and Dennis Viollet were in double seats close by, and Mark Jones, Tommy Taylor, Duncan Edwards and Eddie Colman were all at the back of the aircraft, as were most of the newspapermen.

As we accelerated down the runway, the mood remained relaxed and happy. Most of the footballers were playing cards and close to me I caught sight of the Daily Mail photographer Peter Howard, together with the fellow who had helped him to wire his pictures, a Royal Air Force pilot during the war. But just as we were anticipating the sensation of lift-off there was a frantic screeching of brakes and we slithered to an unexpected halt. We were not offered any explanation as to why this had happened. The pilot simply turned the plane around and taxied back down the runway, then we started off again. This second time he pulled up sooner and far more easily, and it crossed my mind that something might be wrong with the plane. Suddenly I felt uneasy, though still I had complete confidence in the pilots, their procedure and the aircraft itself. After all, they were the professionals.

Peter Howard's wire man looked out of the window and joked that the engine looked as though it could have done with a little more elastic. I guess that was typical stiff-upper-lip stuff you might expect from a former pilot. But Big Frank Swift, the former Manchester City and England goalkeeping legend who now made his living as a writer, leapt to his feet at the back of the plane and roared out: 'What the hell's going on here?' At last there was some communication. We were told there was a technical fault, that we were returning to the terminal for it to be sorted out, and that there was expected to be only a slight delay. So everybody got off and some of the pressmen made calls. Once again poor Mrs Miklos was dashing about dispensing coffee, though most of us didn't have time to drink it before we were herded, like sheep, out to the plane for the final time. It seems ghoulish to recall, now, but some of us were joking about crashing, making remarks along the lines of 'Well, this is it boys.' There was definitely some anxiety in the air. I was trying to remind myself how much I enjoyed flying.

Yet again there was a delay, this time because a reporter, Alf Clarke from the Manchester Evening Chronicle, had hurried away to telephone a short story about the hold-up. He was subjected to some good-natured ribbing when he returned, rather breathlessly, and was strapped into his seat. By this time Kenny Morgans and David Pegg had left our little card school. I'm not sure where Kenny sat but David decided that he would be safer at the back of the plane. He went to join Mark Jones, Tommy Taylor and Eddie Colman. It was to prove a fateful decision.

In my mind's eye, I can see the faces of those lads now. Absolutely clearly. As usual Mark was looking a little white around the gills; he didn't enjoy flying and always seemed apprehensive before take-off. Frank Taylor, who was working for the News Chronicle at the time, had been at the back with the other pressmen, but he had moved forward, probably to interview someone, and when he was asked to sit down and strap himself in he did so near the front. That was a strange twist of fate because most of the other newspapermen were killed. Roger Byrne joked that it was all or nothing this time. Billy Whelan, a devout Roman Catholic who might have made an excellent priest, murmured that whatever was coming, he was ready for it.

Then we started to taxi forward again, and I was hit by the strongest possible feeling of foreboding. Something told me that we were not going to make it. It came to me that we should not be attempting to take off this third time in such terrible weather. By this time all the cards had stopped. I crouched right down, jamming my head into my chest, well below the level of the top of the seat, and strapping myself in so tightly that I could hardly breathe. I have little doubt that these precautions saved my life.

As we accelerated down the runway I peered out of the window at the snow racing past. My last memory is of pushing the pack of cards hurriedly into my side pocket. The engines were surging but there was a peculiar note, as though they could not really get going, and the movement of the aircraft seemed decidedly sluggish.

Then, just at the moment when we should have been getting off the ground, there was the first of a series of three sickening bumps. The first must have been the aircraft hitting a perimeter fence, the second when the pilot pulled up his wheels and the third, and loudest, when we hit a house. I just had time to think to myself 'This is it' before I had the sensation of being thrown all over the place. Then there was darkness.

The next thing I knew there was a knocking on the window. Albert Scanlon had disappeared from in front of me but I seemed to be all right, still strapped into my seat. There was absolutely nothing where the right side of the aircraft should have been, where Roger Byrne and company had been sitting. It was open to the sky, the fuselage having been sliced diagonally. I must have missed the break by a few inches. I could so easily have died with the rest of the lads.

A man at the window was yelling at me to get the bloody hell out of there. 'What the hell are you doing in there? Get out, man, get out,' he shouted. I know now that the man was Captain Thain, and that he was trying to fight the fire in a huge engine with a tiny little extinguisher. I attempted to get up and get out but I couldn't. Then I realised I was still wearing the strap so I unbuckled it and then I could move. I scrambled out through a jagged hole in the side of the plane, weaving past shards of twisted metal, and then there came into my mind a vivid picture I had seen so many times in films, that of an engine blowing up after a crash. So I started running and must have covered, oh I don't know, perhaps 50 yards through thick snow, though somehow it didn't seem to touch my feet. When I was out of breath I stopped running and looked around for the first time.

I could not believe the sight which met my eyes. The aircraft was cut in half; it was just a mass of jagged metal. Much worse, bodies were strewn from it in a neat line, and they were in slush and water where the snow had melted. The tail end of the plane appeared to have hit a house or a lorry or both. It was perched on high, looming over them, with burning bushes and drums scattered everywhere. The Union Jack was blazing away on the tail, and that part of the plane was caught up with the truck. The sound of burning was terrible. It took hold of my mind and only gradually did I realise that I was standing with a bunch of confused people, mostly German women. As I walked back towards a scene of utter desolation, wondering what I could do to help, I could see Matt Busby trying to sit up. I spotted Roger Byrne and although there wasn't a mark on him I was sure from the unnatural way that he was sitting that he must be dead. Others I saw were Jackie Blanchflower, Dennis Viollet and Bobby Charlton, who was still strapped into his seat but was unconscious. Johnny Berry was there, too. Presumably they had all been thrown clear by the impact. At that point it crossed my mind that Roger might be the only fatality, with the rest getting away with injuries. If only that had been the case.

Suddenly I realised that, despite having boarded that same plane as my friends, there didn't seem to be a mark on me. I walked nearer in an absolute daze. It was difficult to believe that I had been any part of the crash. Suddenly I saw Harry Gregg walking out of the wreckage, carrying some sort of bundle and calling for help. Then the bundle moved and cried and I realised he had a tiny baby. I hadn't even realised there had been a baby on board. Harry had blood all over his face and I thought he must be badly cut, but actually it turned out that he had only a small nick on his nose. Later it transpired that Harry had shown immense courage, going back into the stricken plane to search for survivors.

I remember kneeling down beside Matt and he kept saying: 'It's my side, it's my side,' in a horrible deep moan. I wrapped him in my coat and sat holding his hand and looking around. At that moment I thought that Harry and I must be the only ones to have come through unscathed. Then a man came rushing by and flung down a stretcher beside the Boss, saying that someone would be coming for it soon. Suddenly, almost surreally, Bobby Charlton woke up, just as if he had been enjoying a nap, and without a word he walked over to us, took off his jacket and put it under Matt, who was still in the slush. Then Dennis Viollet regained consciousness in much the same way, and stretched. By this time Harry was kneeling alongside Jackie Blanchflower, who was groaning. Harry was doing his best to comfort him and showed fantastic presence of mind in applying a tight tourniquet to Jackie's shattered arm. At this point it cheered me up to see so many people stirring. The thought struck me that it was not so bad after all.

Then a man drove up in a Volkswagen minibus from which all the back seats had been removed. We all helped to get the Boss on to the stretcher and load him into the makeshift ambulance. The driver motioned to Bobby and Dennis to get in the front with him while Harry and I took the middle seats. Then we bounced away over the snow, going much too fast for my liking, and I was reaching backwards trying to hold Matt's stretcher steady. This nightmare progress continued until someone ran in front of the van to stop it. Then they loaded Mrs Miklos, who appeared to be very badly burned, into the back and we set off again. Now the driver really put his foot down and we were lurching all over the road, skidding dangerously. I just couldn't stand it. I shouted at him to slow down. What the hell did he think he was doing, trying to kill us all? He just ignored me and kept driving. I couldn't have been thinking clearly because I remember hitting him on the back of his head as hard as I could, but he didn't stop. He just kept on driving, doing his job the best way he knew how. Dennis and Bobby, obviously in deep shock, just sat there with no expression on their faces, as though they were being taken for a pleasant Sunday afternoon drive in the country.

It was only when we reached the hospital that reality started to hit me. The stretchers were rushed in and we sat around for a while. I recall that I had no shoes on and that my stockinged feet made wet marks on the floor. I think I must have eased off my shoes to make myself more comfortable before the plane set off, and I hadn't noticed their absence until now, despite running through the snow.

We were desperate to get in touch with the British Embassy to let our families know that we were still alive, but we couldn't find anyone who could help us. Obviously at home they would have heard news of the disaster and feared the worst. Then all thoughts of that were driven from my mind when someone called me into a ward and asked me if I could identify the little man on the bed. The face was a terrible mess but I recognised Johnny Berry. The people in the hospital were very calm and efficient, but to me everything still seemed to be confused. And I was not the only one. I have vague memories of a Yugoslav who had been on the aircraft with us, who had been dazedly following Harry, Bobby and myself around the hospital corridors. It turned out that he had been trailing about with a broken leg. He, like us, was in a kind of trance.

Suddenly we were approached by a posse of nurses and they were brandishing needles. They wanted us to remain at the hospital but we all protested that we were quite fit. But they got hold of Bobby Charlton, who was the most distracted of us, and they gave him a jab. Before he knew what had happened he was flat out. Harry and I would not have it. We wanted to get away from the hospital, where the atmosphere was troubling us. A girl from BEA appeared, fetched me a pair of shoes – or rather they were high boots – and took us to a hotel in town. From that point Harry and I were almost inseparable until we got back to Manchester. We hated the idea of being alone and left with our thoughts. It seems stupid now but we even went to the toilet together. We sat in the hotel bedroom, not knowing what to do. By that stage of my career I had pretty well given up alcohol, but someone had given us a bottle of whisky and we drank it between us.

During those next few scrambled days, time meant very little. I don't remember day and night, I couldn't sleep and nothing seemed to matter any more. It was as though I was moving through some strange world that was not my own. We just didn't know what was going on, had no idea of the scale of the calamity. Even now, it makes me shudder to think of it. On one occasion, though, I recall going back to the hospital and leaving Harry in the hotel room. I thought I would pop in to see all the lads, just to see how they were getting on, and I couldn't understand why the staff would not let me into the wards.

Captain Thain was there, along with one of the stewardesses, and they were trying to find out exactly who had been in our party and how many there should have been. Eventually I found a list of people who were in that hospital and I asked where the other hospital was. Where had the rest of the team been taken? And it was when they finally impressed upon me that there was no other hospital that the terrible truth dawned on me for the first time. I couldn't believe it, didn't want to believe it. I asked a lady doctor for Bert Whalley, trainer Tom Curry and Walter Crickmer, and she just shook her head. Then I mentioned some of the other players – Eddie Colman, Tommy Taylor, David Pegg, Billy Whelan, Mark Jones, Geoff Bent – and again came that agonising negative. I began to realise how lucky I had been.

The next time we went back to the hospital everyone was very nice to us. The same lady doctor who had consulted me about Johnny Berry took us in to see everyone. They had cleaned up the immediate carnage now and everything was efficiently organised. The wards were small, leading off a main thoroughfare, with about six beds in each one. Matt Busby was in an oxygen tent, looking absolutely terrible, the same pale shade as the wall and breathing through a tube. Frank Taylor, the News Chronicle man, was in the same ward, apparently asleep.

We approached the bed of Duncan Edwards and he was shouting: 'Let's have some bloody attention!' The doctor marvelled at him and said: 'He's a very strong boy.' She reckoned that at that point Duncan had a 50-50 chance of survival, but that Johnny Berry's prospects were no better than 25-75. When I heard that prognosis I believed firmly that Duncan would recover, even if he was never able to play football again. After all, he had never lost a 50-50 challenge in his life. But, oh, how tragically wrong that well-meaning doctor's prediction turned out to be, although in Johnny's case, of course, it was wonderful that she was mistaken.

We saw Captain Rayment, the co-pilot, whose head had been shaved. He had a huge scar across it. On my way out Frank Taylor shouted to me: 'Hey, Foulkesy, aren't you talking to the poor?' I went over to speak to him and he called for a bottle of beer. His leg was in plaster and was strung up high, but he insisted that he was having a smashing time. At that point he had no idea what had happened to all the others. In the end I believe Frank was the last to leave the hospital, where he remained for several months, but eventually he did make a full recovery.

In adjoining wards we came across people who were a little less seriously injured. Jackie Blanchflower, who had been a pretty useful golfer, was fretting about whether his damaged arm would affect his swing. Dennis Viollet, who still looked exceedingly groggy, had suffered a nasty knock to the jaw and a gash on his head. Typically, he was worried whether this might affect his parting! He was always very particular about his appearance. Poor Albert Scanlon was still out of it. He had been found under a wheel, with a fractured skull. I suppose he must have fallen straight through the bottom of the plane. I remembered that he had been sitting opposite me, so close. Why had I been spared?

Nearby there was Ray Wood with a gashed face and concussion, and Bobby Charlton with bandages on his head. Kenny Morgans was there, too. We didn't say much to any of them, the situation was beyond anything but the briefest of words. Basically we just touched them, to give them some comfort, and then let them rest.

It had been a hideous experience but when Harry and I returned to the hotel, at least we had something positive to cling to, the fact that there were some survivors. For all that, we were devastated by the loss of so many chums, and at that time we didn't know that one more was going to die. I must have been in a terrible mental state. I know that I wasn't sleeping or eating properly, and by the time we got home I had lost a stone.

Harry and I were not happy with the idea of our wives flying over to see us in our debilitated condition; neither did we want to subject them to the far worse state of the other survivors. So when the party of wives and relatives was being put together to journey to Munich, we pleaded with them, by telephone, not to come. I managed to convince Mavis – Harry's wife, who has since died – that there was nothing wrong with him and he did likewise with Teresa. Although they did not seem to believe us fully, we managed to make them realise that we would not have been able to ring them if we had been severely injured. I was desperately afraid of them coming over on a plane. I couldn't face the prospect of it.

Eventually, all the wives who did come gathered in our bedroom, and it was a terrible ordeal for everyone concerned. Mrs Busby and her daughter, Sheena, and Johnny Berry's wife impressed me mightily with the absolute calm with which they approached the whole ghastly business. I remember Duncan Edwards' mate, Jimmy, and his girl, Molly. There was Jackie's wife, Jean; Dennis' wife, Barbara; and Albert's wife, Josephine, who was expecting a baby; they were all in our room, all very upset and trying not to show it.

Sooner or later – I can't remember when exactly – Jimmy Murphy appeared on the scene. Clearly he was horrendously shaken, utterly demoralised, but he put on a brave show and tried to joke for our benefit. I remember going out to the toilet and seeing poor Jimmy sitting all hunched up on the stairs, his head in his hands as if his world had crumbled about him. The shock to him must have been monumental. He had missed the trip to Belgrade because he had been away in charge of Wales for a World Cup qualifier. These boys were like sons to him and now so many of them were snatched away. The story goes that when he reached Duncan's bed, Duncan assured Jimmy that he would be fit for the Wolves game on Saturday and asked the kick-off time. That really must have broken Jimmy up.

All the time, newspapermen were clamouring to know the full story of the crash and eventually we went to their hotel and tried to tell them exactly what had happened or, to be more accurate, what we thought had happened. By this time the stewardess who had been looking after Harry and myself was completely exhausted, but she took us out again to buy some clothes. I had lost an overcoat and I bought an expensive one in Munich, though it didn't fit me properly because I had lost so much weight.

It might have been Friday, but might just as easily have been Saturday, when we were taken back to the scene of the accident. A German official quizzed both Harry and myself. I seem to remember that Mr Anthony Millward, who went on to become head of BEA, was there, too. We decided to have a look around the wreckage, which was strewn over a wide area. I got back into the part of the plane where I had been sitting, which was a weird sensation. To my amazement I found the bottle of gin which had been given to me at the post-match Embassy party. Also there were my briefcase full of magazines and my overcoat, jammed up against the roof, still in the rack and totally undamaged.

Someone took a picture of me clambering out of the plane clutching the gin. As we rummaged around, I found a presentation cap with Eddie Colman's name on it and his scarf. This upset me so much I could stand it no longer. Then Jimmy, Duncan's friend, started shouting that he had found what looked like a valuable diamond ring and a lot more jewellery. The German official sent for an armed policeman, who was left to guard the wreckage. It turned out that the jewellery belonged to poor Mrs Miklos. Another official took us back into the airport building and gave us a welcome stiff drink before we went to look through the rest of the luggage which had been salvaged. Ironically, the cases of the men who had been killed seemed to be largely intact. One briefcase, lying forlornly on its own, turned out to be bulging with cash and travellers cheques.

After one more visit to the hospital, where things were beginning to look blacker than ever for some of the badly injured, Jimmy Murphy decided wisely that we would be better off at home. He was brilliant, telling us not to bother about football. But we all knew that, sometime soon, we would have to begin thinking about the future of Manchester United. Unbelievably the airline officials were stupid enough to ask us to fly back to Manchester at their expense. My reaction was unequivocal. I told them they would never get me in a stinking plane again. But, as it turned out, it was just as bad on the train. Every time we braked I got into a terrible panic, almost a frenzy, coming out in a sweat and shaking uncontrollably. I felt as though I was living through the aircrash all over again. I understand now that I should have been back there in that hospital with Bobby Charlton, under treatment for shock, but all I wanted at that moment was to get the hell out of Munich.

I know it was an illusion but we seemed to be travelling for days, Harry, Jimmy and I in one compartment. In Holland a little Chinaman passed us in the corridor and Jimmy, doing his utmost to cheer us up, said that we had better sign him on. We might need him! In fact, there was a lot of truth in that little joke. Obviously, on the way home we gave some thought to the future and Jimmy told me that I would have to be captain for the next match. He didn't ask me, he just told me. It was almost impossible to address the idea of playing football, though, and on the boat to Harwich I got into a worse state than ever, thinking that we were never going to make it. All I wanted to know was where they kept the lifeboats and the lifejackets.

An army of photographers was waiting for us at the dock, but because we had hardly any luggage we went straight through customs. I had never been scared of anything in my life before, but the train to London went so fast that I was sorely tempted to pull the communication cord and make a run for it. My mind was taken off the journey for a while when a man called Hubert Gregg introduced himself to Harry, saying that he was the actor, and wanting to know where Harry hailed from. He was extremely sympathetic and kind, explaining that he was not a relation, but always liked to know about anyone who shared his name. He wished us all the best and we went out to face the largest collection of photographers I had ever seen – and I had seen a few awesome press gatherings in my time. Harry and Jimmy stepped out first and I managed to sidle out behind the crush without being noticed.

Immediately the journalists had Harry up against a wall and were grilling him, but I didn't feel like facing that so I asked a policeman the way and I fled. I must have a knack of doing that.

Teresa and Mavis were waiting for Harry and myself at the hotel and there was a tearful reunion during which we learnt of the different sort of ordeal the girls had gone through. It seems that Teresa had learned of the accident from a neighbour and then had to wait nearly an hour for the next news bulletin – there was no 24-hour news service in those days. Even then she did not know whether I was a survivor or not, and together with Mavis she was whisked off to London by a Mirror reporter, who put them up in a hotel. At that point, though she had been told I was alive, reliable information remained scarce, and the pair of them went to a cinema, just to get an update from a newsreel. Obviously, they were worried sick.

After comparing notes, we all set off for Manchester in a huge Rolls-Royce. Once again I could not cope with the speed at which we were being driven and kept telling the driver to slow down. Much later I was told that he had been going really slowly, almost dawdling along, but it didn't seem like that to me. It took me a very long time to get over the fear of travelling; in particular, I just could not abide braking.

The doctors told me I should have a long holiday away from it all, but how could I? I couldn't stop thinking of poor Jimmy Murphy, trying to keep the ship afloat at Old Trafford. I remember him saying that we would have to find a trainer, before anything else, now that Tom Curry was gone. I suggested Jack Crompton, United's former goalkeeper who I knew was doing a very good job for Luton Town at that time. To be honest, I doubted whether he would come but Jack jumped at the chance and remained with United for many more years, even resisting the temptation of the Luton manager's chair when it was offered to him subsequently.

My strangest souvenir of Munich was the pack of playing cards that I had slipped into my pocket shortly before the impact. I had not the slightest bruise on me, and my pocket was not ripped, yet the top quarter-inch of those cards had been sliced off and had disappeared. The cut was so clean it looked as if it might have been made by a razor. How they came to be like that was a total mystery.

As to the reasons for the disaster, there are various theories. At first it was thought the cause was a build-up of ice on the wings and that was the conclusion reached by no less than three official inquiries, two German and one British. Initially a lot of the blame was attached to Captain Thain but he never believed in the iced-up wings theory and fought tirelessly to clear his name. It was not until 1969 that he succeeded when a fourth inquiry endorsed his belief that the plane had been prevented from taking off by slush on the runway. He has since died.

I know I was incredibly fortunate to walk out of that plane physically unscathed, but more than 40 years later I am still suffering the mental scars from the crash. If such a thing happened today we'd all be counselled incessantly, but there was nothing of that sort in 1958. We just had to get on with life.

Since then, although I have flown all over the world on a routine basis in my work as a coach, I've turned down countless opportunities because of my aversion to flying. Before Munich I loved to fly; afterwards I loathed it; my confidence was shredded. Even now I suffer agonies of anxiety for a week before I fly and I suffer painful after-effects from every flight. The images of that day never, never leave me. I have gone through them time and again as I have travelled the world.

Of course, I am not the only one. It must apply to all the survivors. Certainly I saw it in Albert Scanlon in 1998 when we were taken back to Munich, where the European Cup Final was being played, to mark the fortieth anniversary of the disaster. Looking at Albert, who had never flown since that day, I could see that he was going through agony as he clutched his seat in terror. He travelled home by train and I don't blame him. We were lucky that we didn't lose our lives, but we lost a lot of other things. Should more have been done to help us, both at the time and since then? Yes, I think it should.

# Eight

# Rising from the ashes

THE AFTERMATH of Munich was a grim and grievous time for everyone connected with Manchester United. The first few days offered nothing more than blank misery, with a heart-rending round of funerals, although I didn't attend any of them. There was no way I could have faced that ordeal. I had been deeply disturbed by the crash and the services would have upset me so much that I doubt if I'd ever have played football again. It was imperative to me that I escape the emotional, near-hysterical atmosphere which had built up in Manchester, and although nothing could put the world to rights, Jimmy Murphy offered the best solution possible by taking the fit senior players, plus a collection of youngsters, away to the Norbreck Hotel in Blackpool to prepare somehow for the immediate future. Despite the enormity of the tragedy, United had to go on, and although the League and FA had given permission for the postponement of fixtures in the short term, a cup tie against Sheffield Wednesday at Old Trafford was fixed for February 19, just 13 days after the disaster. So we virtually lived at the Norbreck and I didn't see Teresa for more than a day each week over the next six weeks, as we strove to keep the club afloat, to forge new team spirit from what remained of the first-team squad, plus a couple of emergency signings and an eager but painfully green selection of reserves.

Unquestionably these were the darkest days of my footballing life, and they passed in a blur. But something which remains crystal clear from that period is the almost superhuman strength and resilience of Jimmy Murphy, as he took on the gargantuan task of keeping Manchester United afloat. In those early weeks, as poor Matt hovered between life and death in a German hospital, Jimmy was an inspiration. The boys who had died had been like sons to him, and he was devastated on a purely personal level, never mind about football. How he survived emotionally I will never know, especially after the death of Duncan nearly two weeks after the accident. Our deputy manager had always had a soft spot for our seemingly indestructible young giant and when news came through that the boy had passed on, I just don't know how Jimmy coped. It was yet another crushing blow on top of so many, not least the loss of his close friend and fellow coach Bert Whalley. I, too, could hardly believe that Bert was gone. He had been like a father to me in my early days as a Red Devil, firm but invariably kindly and incredibly knowledgeable about the game.

Another chronic loss in the crash was Tom Curry, a fine man and a splendid trainer, now replaced by old comrade Jack Crompton. Thus reinforced, but still carrying what must have seemed like the weight of the world on his shoulders, Jimmy Murphy set about the task of ensuring the survival of the club – and against all the odds, he prevailed.

Jimmy was a firebrand of a motivator who lifted men by his sheer passion, but he was an articulate fellow, too, a cute psychologist in his own way, and well-loved by all of us. In the past he had been the perfect foil for Matt, the two of them bouncing ideas off each other as they attempted to get the best out of an exceptionally talented squad of players. Now he found himself in sole charge of a team which was far from first-rate and, despite the crushingly tragic circumstances, the weight of expectation must have been immense. One of the biggest problems was that, no matter how dire the straits we were in, other clubs did not want to let us have their good players. There was talk that we might recruit Ferenc Puskas, Hungary's famous 'Galloping Major' and one of the all-time greats, but nothing came of that, and rumours about Jeff Whitefoot, our former midfielder, and Bolton full-back Tommy Banks also proved incorrect. However, we did manage two signings. Jimmy and I went to Blackpool to talk to veteran schemer Ernie Taylor, who had recently experienced his own tragedy with the loss of his seven-year-old son in a car accident. His wife said she was glad we had arrived because he needed taking out of himself and it was obvious straight away that he was keen to join us. He was well past his best but still had brilliant skills and was a great organiser. We just gave him the ball and he set things up for us; Ernie turned out to be a marvellous short-term acquisition. The other newcomer was Stan Crowther, a mightily abrasive wing-half who had played against us for Aston Villa in the 1957 FA Cup Final, but although he helped us through the rest of that traumatic season, he never really fitted in.

As for myself, I was in a dreadful state, both physically and mentally. Understandably in the circumstances, Jimmy told me that I had to be captain. I was never going to refuse but the job carried added pressure which I was in no position to take. Everything was getting too much for me and, in all honesty, the last thing I wanted to do was to play football. I wasn't eating or sleeping properly and I was losing weight rapidly. I guess I was teetering on the brink of some sort of breakdown, but had no appreciation of that at the time. When I look back now at the picture of myself leading the team out to face Sheffield Wednesday in that first match after the disaster, I resemble a ghost. I'm sure that it was only my high level of fitness beforehand which carried me through, but I was no more than a shadow of my true self.

The team which followed me out was unrecognisable from our pre-Munich line-up, with only Harry and myself able to retain our places. Partnering me at full-back was Ian Greaves, while the half-back line consisted of Freddie Goodwin, Ronnie Cope and Stan Crowther. Colin Webster filled the right-wing slot, Ernie Taylor was joined in the inside trio by teenagers Alex Dawson and Mark Pearson, while rawest of all was Shay Brennan, a young wing-half cum inside-forward deployed on the left flank. Of the crash survivors, Berry and Blanchflower would never play again; Viollet, Charlton and Morgans would not return until later in the campaign; and Scanlon and Wood would not see senior action until the following term.

We had done our best to remain cheerful on the bus from the Norbreck, but when we reached the ground the atmosphere was unnerving, somehow unnatural. Such was the communal grief that the supporters seemed to be on the edge of their nerves, and throughout the evening the feeling in the air became ever-more emotional, eventually verging on hysteria, a constant hum whatever the state of the game. I felt sorry for the Wednesday players, whose body language made it evident that they didn't know how to handle the situation. Their skipper was Albert Quixall, soon to become an Old Trafford team-mate, and a friend of several of the United lads who had died. I could see it in his eyes that he would rather have been anywhere else that night. Sheffield Wednesday were a fine, strong team at the time, and on paper they should have thrashed an inexperienced combination such as ours, but they didn't have the heart for this particular FA Cup fifth round tie. They knew that everyone in the country, with the possible exception of their own fans, were willing United to win, and we did so rather easily in the end with Shay Brennan emerging as an unlikely two-goal hero. Alex Dawson grabbed the other in a 3-0 victory which brought me precious little elation. I did my best to bear up, but basically it didn't seem right to be playing football at that point.

That put us into the quarter-finals, where we faced West Bromwich Albion, another accomplished side who might have expected little trouble in disposing of an under-strength United. However, now we were riding a tidal wave of public fervour which, it seemed, would not be denied, and with Jimmy Murphy an uplifting figure, we rose to the challenge with a pulsating 2-2 draw at the Hawthorns, courtesy of strikes from Dawson and man-of-the-match Ernie Taylor. In fact, we almost won at the first attempt, with Albion claiming a late and controversial equaliser, and I remember reflecting that a golden chance had passed us by. Yet the replay proved even more extraordinary, with the Midlanders putting us under constant pressure for the first 87 minutes before Ronnie Cope, who had performed majestically throughout, launching a long clearance from which a typical burst of Bobby Charlton magic set up a dramatic winner for Colin Webster. In all honesty, we didn't deserve it on the run of play, we were outclassed, but some unseen hand appeared to be guiding us towards Wembley.

Meanwhile, predictably enough, we were struggling in the League, registering only a single win between the accident and season's end, but that didn't seem to matter as we prepared for a semi-final against Second Division Fulham at Villa Park. This time a lot of people made us the favourites – which I thought was daft – but, with England midfield general Johnny Haynes in tremendous form, they pushed us all the way. In fact, it took a late strike from Bobby Charlton, his second of the match, to earn us a replay at Highbury. I don't know how I got through that game as I was suffering from flu as well as ongoing debilitation from the crash. I felt seriously ill but I knew there was no way I could duck out as were were down to a skeleton crew already. In the event the Fulham return was a classic and we won it 5-3 thanks to a hat-trick from Dawson and goals from Bobby and Shay. Although we were in London, the crowd was solidly behind United, and I shall always remember the magnaminity of Haynes after the final whistle, presenting us with the champagne which had been put on ice for Fulham.

Now, incredibly, our patchwork team had defied all known odds to reach Wembley. In truth we had relied heavily on the brilliance and authority of Harry Gregg, while hitherto unknown youngsters such as Dawson and Mark Pearson had grown immeasurably in stature. Unfortunately, being pushed so hard so soon – as they had to be – might have done their careers lasting harm. Both of them had the ability to become established at Old Trafford but neither did so, and although they did well enough elsewhere, they must always wonder what heights they might have attained had they been able to develop at a more natural pace.

Having reached the FA Cup Final, and for the second successive season, we were desperate to win, but Wembley proved to be one game too far, even for Murphy's Marvels, as we became known. Though I couldn't begin to show it, I was thoroughly depressed, all the weeks of unbearable strain had caught up with me, and I understand now that I needed expert help. In those days, though, you just got on with it. Bobby must have been suffering similarly, yet he had played brilliantly in the months after being thrown out of that wrecked aircraft, while Dennis did not return to action until April. Jimmy gambled on Viollet's fitness at Wembley but it is clear, in retrospect, that our star marksman was anything but ready for such a demanding occasion.

In the run-up to the big game against Bolton Wanderers – in which I would face my childhood pal, Derek Hennin – I felt a sense of impending gloom, despite the almost superhuman efforts of Jimmy Murphy, whose astonishing achievement in guiding us to the twin towers has to be one of the all-time sporting miracles, especially given the fact that our fixture backlog had forced us to play no fewer than 13 times between March 22 and April 26. Even the presence at Wembley of Matt Busby, who had been making a painfully slow recovery from the injuries he had received at Munich, did not cheer me up. He was hobbling along on a walking stick, looking bent, grey and very old, and the sight of him, together with unavoidable memories of friends I would never see again, added to my sombre mood. This was heightened still further by the moving strains of 'Abide With Me', which drifted into the dressing room, though walking out on to Wembley's lush turf and breathing in lungfuls of fresh air did make me feel better. The team I led out consisted of Harry Gregg, myself at right-back, Ian Greaves, Freddie Goodwin, Ronnie Cope, Stan Crowther, Alex Dawson, Ernie Taylor, Bobby Charlton, Dennis Viollet and Colin Webster. The unluckiest fellow to miss out was Mark Pearson, who had excelled on the road to the final and whom I would have selected in place of the below-par Viollet. Meanwhile another who had contributed to the post-Munich cup run, Shay Brennan, would resurface triumphantly as a classy full-back and enjoy his own moment in the Wembley sun some ten years later.

For all the drama which was to attend the Bolton clash, it was a hugely undistinguished game which got off to a dreaful start for us when a speculative effort from Bryan Edwards was deflected into the path of Nat Lofthouse, who netted at his leisure from five yards. Thereafter Bolton always looked the more powerful unit, though Bobby Charlton threatened periodically and he had just rattled Eddie Hopkinson's post with a trademark rasper when United became the victims of another Wembley goalkeeping outrage. The ball switched to the other end and Dennis Stevens, ironically a cousin of Duncan Edwards, let fly with a fierce shot which Harry Gregg could only push into the air. As the Irishman caught the dropping ball, Lofthouse barged into him with all his might, his leading shoulder catching Harry in the middle of his back; goalkeeper and ball were deposited unceremoniously into the net and, unbelievably, the referee signalled a goal. Unquestionably it was a foul, as Nat himself has since admitted. Even in those days, when more physical contact was allowed, you could not get away with that. The decision was wrong, an absolute shambles, and it finished any impetus that we might have been building. That said, Bolton were the better team on the day, but it was so galling, especially after coming so far and in such uniquely taxing circumstances, to lose out in such an unjust manner.

After that there was never a friendly atmosphere when we played Bolton, although I refute any suggestion that there was a vendetta. Later, when I marked Nat, Matt told me to keep tight to him, give him no room, but never to attempt to hurt him. Inevitably there were collisions and in one game, as he picked himself up for perhaps the sixth time, he said to me: 'I'm getting bloody tired of this. Have you got it out of your system now?' But he never complained or argued beyond that. He accepted that I wasn't retaliating for the cup final, merely playing the game on that day the best way that I knew how. Still, I wouldn't be honest if I didn't admit that the Wembley episode rankled, although many years later the principal protagonists could have a laugh about it – occasionally at my expense. I recall a function not too many years ago when Teresa came upon Harry and Nat chatting, and she said to the Irishman: 'I don't know how you can talk to him after what he did to you.' Harry's reply was instant: 'What Nat did was nothing compared to some of the things I've seen your husband do!'

Amazingly, even the FA Cup Final did not bring down the curtain on that epic, tragic, seemingly never-ending season of 1957/58. Though it had become somewhat obscured by subsequent events, way back in February, in the last match before Munich, we had qualified to meet AC Milan in the semi-final of the European Cup, the first leg of which we played only five days after our disappointment against Bolton.

On the face of it our threadbare side had little chance against the Italian aristocrats, but what a fright we gave them at Old Trafford! After the skilful Uruguayan, Schiaffino, had put them in front deservedly after 24 minutes, we dug in and fought as if our lives depended on it, and five minutes before the break Viollet levelled following a mishit back-pass by Cesare Maldini. In the second half we stormed forward in waves, but just when it looked as if we would have to settle for a draw, Maldini baulked Viollet and little Ernie Taylor, unmoved by the concerted Italian protests which greeted the referee's penalty decision, coolly rapped home the spot-kick via the crossbar. It was a sensational victory for which I don't believe our team has received due credit down the years. For the likes of Goodwin, Cope, Webster and Pearson – bolstered by the temporary return of Morgans but deprived of Bobby Charlton by the FA's barely believable refusal to release him from England duty – to triumph against such illustrious opponents in a European Cup semi-final was overwhelmingly glorious. It deserves an honoured place in the annals of the game, and its merit should not be reduced by our subsequent

4-0 collapse in the second leg in Milan. By then we had run out of emotional steam, and were completely drained. To be honest, it's an occasion which I have tried for many years to shut out of my mind. The Italian supporters, about 80,000 of them, showed not one jot of compassion for the trauma we had endured in recent months and we were bombarded with vegetables as we walked into the San Siro arena. I remember being struck by a shower of cabbages and the biggest bunch of carrots I had ever seen. They hurt, too. The hostility was accentuated by an endless barrage of flares and fireworks and, in truth, we were never really in contention against top-quality opponents. It was a sad, anti-climactic end to an horrific interlude in my life, but I suppose it was inevitable. Sheer spirit and raw emotion had kept us going for a long time, but eventually it was not enough. Afterwards my overriding feeling was one of relief at being able to rest, and I thanked my lucky stars that I was still playing football when so many of my old friends were gone.

The following season, Jimmy handed the reins back to Matt and resumed his role as the faithful lieutenant. He had been a tower of strength throughout the post-Munich period and it saddens me to say that I don't think the club ever fully appreciated the extent of his input, or what it took out of him both physically and mentally. His loyalty was illustrated soon afterwards when he spurned the chance of managing Arsenal to continue working alongside Matt at Old Trafford, and while his sheer quality was never in doubt, he emphasised it spectacularly by leading Wales to the quarter-finals of the World Cup only a few months on from the air crash. Manchester United should understand, and never lose sight of the fact, that Jimmy Murphy, who died in 1989, goes down as one of the most loyal, dedicated and inspirational contributors to their cause in their entire history. His memory deserves to be honoured like few others.

# Nine

## The road back

**M**UCH IS made, and quite justly, of the post-Munich Red Devils' astonishing achievement in reaching the 1958 FA Cup Final, but I believe that an even more Herculean feat tends to be almost criminally underestimated. In 1958/59 we finished as runners-up in the Championship race with a side which was, with all due respects, still little more than an emergency combination, stitched together hastily in the aftermath of the crash.

With Matt Busby on the mend but still far from fully functional at the start of the campaign, it was the heroic Jimmy Murphy who set the tone once more, preaching a non-stop sermon of togetherness. 'Defend in strength, attack in strength' was Jimmy's motto, and we followed it to the letter. However, I have to admit that while the rearguard did its bit, with Harry Gregg consistently showing the form that had earned him recognition as the outstanding goalkeeper of the 1958 World Cup Finals, it was our forward line of Warren Bradley, Albert Quixall, Dennis Viollet, Bobby Charlton and Albert Scanlon which made us special that term. We scored more than a century of League goals and played some of the most dazzlingly attractive, free-flowing, fast-moving football it has ever been my pleasure to witness.

With Tommy Taylor gone, there was no big man to act as spearhead, so Dennis became a roaming number-nine, more of a team player than ever before, working ceaselessly off the ball and putting his immense experience to optimum use. He continued to score plenty, of course, but what impressed me the most was the vast number he set up for others, especially Bobby Charlton, who contributed his best-ever total of 29 First Division strikes.

We all changed after the crash, but the difference was most vividly apparent in Bobby, in whose personality there seemed to be a material diffence. Though never by any means an extrovert, now his happy-go-lucky days had truly gone; he was quieter, more withdrawn, apparently less able to express himself. He became a more complex character; sometimes he would greet you and sometimes he wouldn't. Some people thought he had become aloof, but I never believed that. It was as though something was going on inside his head that he couldn't quite bring out, and his attitude was widely misinterpreted. I wasn't a particularly close friend of his, but I feel I understood him, and his need to pull back at times after the tragedy. I think he matured very quickly as a result of Munich; he felt that he should assume more responsibility, and he did just that, but at what personal cost no one but he can truly know. I felt he wanted and needed to be a leader of the players at that time, and eventually he became captain, but not before many others – myself, Dennis Viollet, Maurice Setters, Noel Cantwell and Denis Law – had all had a go at the job. On the pitch, though, he was sensational, playing at inside-left and forming a fabulously effective and entertaining partnership with Dennis.

At inside-right was Albert Quixall, a thoroughbred footballer for whom Matt had broken the British transfer record in September 1958, paying Sheffield Wednesday £45,000 for the England international, whom he saw as the ideal replacement for veteran schemer Ernie Taylor. Albert had been a golden boy at Hillsborough, superbly skilful and a marvellous athlete, and although he never quite realised his full long-term potential at Old Trafford, he made a significant impact in 1958/59. After enduring a difficult settling-in period in which he suffered plenty of unwarranted criticism by pundits – United lost all of his first six games – he produced some sparkling displays, his passing and movement a joy to behold.

That exceptionally gifted inside trio was complemented perfectly by a pair of direct, sharp-shooting wingers, the explosive Albert Scanlon, who netted 16 times from the left, and newcomer Warren Bradley, who scored 12 times in 24 outings on the right. We knew all about Albert already, but Warren arrived like a bolt from the blue, one of several amateurs recruited from Bishop Auckland when we were chronically short of resources after the crash. Though he didn't have the outright class of Johnny Berry, he was similar in many ways – quick, strong, aggressive and industrious – and he did a fabulous holding job for the club. In fact, so naturally did Warren take to United's number-seven shirt that within 15 months of his arrival he had earned full England caps to add to his amateur international honours. His long-term future was in teaching – he became a highly successful headmaster in Manchester – but his fleeting contribution to the Reds' cause was notable.

On paper, Harry Gregg and myself apart, our defence was pretty inexperienced, but both Ian Greaves and a quiet, efficient Irish lad, Joe Carolan, turned in long competent spells at full-back while our usual half-back line of Freddie Goodwin, Ronnie Cope and Wilf McGuinness performed with admirable consistency. So what about me? Well, for all our success in attaining second place to Stan Cullis' Wolves, our closest rivals throughout most of the 1950s, I was far from happy during the first two-thirds of the campaign, which I spent at right-back. In retrospect it's clear that I was suffering some kind of delayed trauma from the accident.

For a start, I didn't want to be captain, though I accept that, as the senior professional at that point, I was the obvious man for Matt to choose. All my life I have been confident, I have believed in myself, but for some time after Munich I was a different person. Doubt had crept in and, even when a sparkling mid-season run of eight successive wins kept us in touch with the leaders, I was not satisfied with my personal form. As a defender I liked to dominate my immediate opponent, but somehow I had become tentative, anything but commanding. It reached a point where there were whispers that

I needed a change of club, and I understand that Liverpool made a tentative inquiry.

While Matt was having none of that, he did recognise that all was not well, and the situation came to a head when our victorious sequence was ended by Newcastle, who earned a 4-4 draw at Old Trafford after being 4-1 down. After the game, he called me in and suggested that I needed a rest, which was the truth although I didn't realise it at the time. I was mortified, and a little bit fearful that my days at United might be numbered. Matt tried to calm my anxieties, and even planted the seed that my future might lie in my favoured position of centre-half, although I felt that was little more than a sop when he told me. As I left his office I couldn't have been more down in the dumps, but I was utterly determined not to give up. I took a long, cool look at myself and understood, deep down, that I had not been doing myself justice. It came home to me that I had never regained the stone in weight I had lost immediately after the crash, and that I was nowhere near optimum fitness. Now, having been given a break from football, I decided that I would do something about it. So I trained for longer hours than ever, ate well and got plenty of early nights, and after several weeks of that demanding self-imposed regime I began to feel a new man. Soon I resumed playing in five-a-side matches in club sessions and I began to feel the bite returning to my game. The timing was back in the tackles, I was heading the ball really well and I felt sharp in a way I had almost forgotten about.

Matt noted the transformation and proved as good as his word, drafting me into the reserve team at centre-half. I took to it immediately, relishing the fact of being at the core of the defence, invariably facing attacks four-square instead of feeling isolated on the flank. But just as everything was slotting into place, and I was harbouring ambitions of a realistic challenge for a first-team berth, my impetus was interrupted in bizarre fashion during a routine encounter with Chesterfield reserves. As I tossed up with the opposing skipper before the game, the referee said to me: 'Any trouble from you, Foulkes, and you're off!' I thought; 'What the hell's going on?' and the Chesterfield captain was clearly puzzled, too, because although I had a reputation as a hard player, I had never received a booking in my life.

That record didn't last for many minutes. however. A high cross came into our goalmouth and I went for it, perfectly fairly, along with their centre-forward. There was no physical contact but he stumbled and, to my astonishment, the referee cautioned me for dangerous play. Then, a few moments later, I leapt to meet a loose ball on halfway, collided accidentally with a forward, and we both finished flat on our backs. The referee, who had been some 40 yards away, ran up, took my name again and sent me off! I was absolutely dumbfounded and so was Jimmy Murphy, who was turning the air blue on the touchline. I had never been in any sort of trouble before and, even though my treatment had been outrageously unjust, I felt terrible about it. For all my total innocence, I hardly relished the prospect of explaining matters to Matt Busby back at Old Trafford, and sure enough he opened the subsequent inquest by declaring that such behaviour 'was very unlike you, Bill'.

However, I knew I had been the victim of a refereeing outrage and there was no way I was going to take the consequence, which would have been the loss of two weeks' wages. I announced that I was not going to let the official get away with such a diabolical decision and that I wanted a personal hearing. Jimmy Murphy supported me to the hilt and we enlisted the help of the Professional Footballers Association. It turned out I was one of the first players to be represented by Jimmy Hill, who proved a resourceful, eloquent and effective advocate. Having satisfied himself of the facts of the Chesterfield incident, he built up a dossier on the referee, discovering that he had dismissed no less than seven United players at Central League level. In those days, when sendings-off were comparatively rare, that was remarkable, and it was additionally amazing that nobody had picked up on what was clearly a personal vendetta against the club. In the event, the case against me was thrown out, there was not a stain on my character, and the referee was suspended sine die.

I was delighted by that result, and although the disruption to my comeback plans had been considerable, I did not let it play on my mind. Duly my improved form earned me first-team selection, in that coveted number-five shirt, for the season's last five games. Although we were beaten on the final day, we had finished pretty strongly, six points adrift of Wolves, but five ahead of third-placed Arsenal. For a side in the early stages of transition, it represented an eminently acceptable return for our endeavour and, although I had not yet made the pivot's position my own, I had laid down a valuable marker for the future. In addition, much to my own satisfaction if not that of Matt Busby at the time, I had rid myself of the captaincy, which had become a burden, affecting my game adversely.

What lay ahead were several years of consolidation and restructuring, with the Boss bringing in some half-a-dozen high-quality players and deciding which of the home-grown recruits would make the grade, before we were ready for a renewed tilt at the game's top honours. During that period of painstaking regrowth, we could hardly hope to maintain our high-riding League status of 1958/59, but I feel our finishes of seventh in both 1959/60 and 1960/61 were acceptable in the circumstances, and while our 15th and 19th of the subsequent two campaigns were disappointing, I believed all along that we were making progress.

Those who showed rich promise but who didn't go on to greater things with United included Johnny Giles, an intelligent, outspoken Dubliner, who displayed phenomenal ability and knowledge of the game for one so young. I thought he couldn't miss becoming a top United star as a play-making inside-forward, but such was the level of competition that he found himself consigned to the right wing too much for his liking. I'm sure that he and the manager had several forthright discussions on that point, and perhaps it was not possible for two such strong characters to agree to disagree. Whatever, the upshot was that Johnny was allowed to join Leeds, with whom he excelled for many seasons under Don Revie. I always thought it was a crying shame that he was transferred; to me he was exactly the type of player we needed in the long term. I'll always think of Johnny Giles as a Manchester United footballer.

When I name just some of the other lads who enjoyed a taste of first-team football at Old Trafford, only to be dispensed with, it makes me realise just how lucky I was, with my limited natural ability, to have such a marathon stint as a Red Devil. Good young players who were nurtured by United but who slipped away in the early 1960s include cultured centre-half Ronnie Cope, skilful wing-halves Freddie Goodwin, Jimmy Nicholson and Nobby Lawton, talented inside-forwards Mark Pearson and Phil Chisnall, mercurial winger Ian Moir, and combative marksmen Alex Dawson and Sammy McMillan.

In addition there were seemingly premature departures for two hugely gifted flankmen who were in the side at the time of Munich, Albert Scanlon and Kenny Morgans. Under normal circumstances, both might have gone on to brilliant careers but, possibly due to delayed psychological effects of the accident, the pair of them lost momentum instead of scaling the loftier peaks for which they had appeared to be destined.

But the man whose exit perturbed me the most was Dennis Viollet, who was sold to Stoke City for £25,000 in January 1962, when he was only 28 and had not long made his full England international debut. As recently as 1959/60 he had smashed the club's seasonal scoring record with 32 strikes in 36 League matches – a mark which still stands at the time of writing, though Ruud van Nistelrooy might have it in his sights – and, in my opinion, there was no facet of forward play that he lacked. I missed him not only for his fabulous input to the team, but also for his friendship, which I had enjoyed for a decade. His sense of humour could be merciless, though. When I complimented him on his enhanced work-rate after Munich, he replied: 'You're a changed man, too, Foulkesy; you're meaner and nastier than ever before!' Cheers, Dennis.

Of course, it was not all one-way traffic at Old Trafford. The exodus was balanced by the steady arrival of proven high-class performers, starting with the ball-winning wing-half Maurice Setters from West Bromwich Albion in January 1960. Maurice was a tremendous competitor and a combative character – occasionally towards team-mates as well as the opposition! – and he did extremely well for United, both in midfield and alongside me in the centre of defence. Certainly, after I became the regular centre-half early in 1960/61, I was always happy to line up with such a doughty warrior as my partner. Maurice was an uncompromising defender, efficient enough to have played his part in the glories that were to follow later in the decade, but he did not always play to his strengths. He was hard and dominating, but sometimes he wanted to be creative, and when he got carried away with fancy footwork which was not his forte, ultimately it cost him his place in the team.

Another major acquisition was full-back Noel Cantwell, signed from West Ham United for £29,500 in November 1960. Already widely respected for his achievements with the Hammers and the Republic of Ireland, Noel was exactly the type of person needed by any football club. Although he was by no means as talented as his countryman John Carey, there were marked similarities between the two. Both were intelligent and articulate, oozing integrity and charm, natural leaders both on and off the pitch. Soon Noel became captain, making such a good fist of it that there was even talk that he might one day succeed Matt as the manager, though that never came to pass. As a player he could attack and create, though sometimes he could seem a bit ponderous in movement, and he was unlucky that two such fine full-backs as Tony Dunne and Shay Brennan were on the rise during the early 1960s. Still, Noel provided stability at a time United needed it urgently, and he continued as club skipper even after losing his place in the team. Noel and his wife, Margaret, became close friends, too, and Teresa was godmother to their son.

A third crucial arrival was that of centre-forward David Herd from Arsenal in the summer of 1961. For half a decade he had been a proven scorer with the Gunners and he carried on his splendid work at Old Trafford. David wasn't a spectacular performer, but he guaranteed 20 goals a season, often striking from distance, explosively and with practically no apparent backlift. He was brave and hard-working, too, and certainly he deserved far more credit than he ever received. In fact, because he wasn't seen as a star, as such, the crowd gave him a hard ride at first, which was terribly unfair. In the end, though, anyone who knew the game came to appreciate his huge worth and he was sorely missed when his United career was curtailed following a broken leg.

But the transfer which really galvanised Manchester United was that of Denis Law, for whom Matt Busby shattered the transfer record again in August 1962. Denis cost £115,000 from the Italian club, Torino, and he was worth every last penny. Until he arrived we could hold our own with most opponents, but if we met a team which was pretty well equal, we lacked that vital spark which would make the difference. Denis provided that, he took us to the next level. As Teresa once put it aptly: 'The game always seemed more exciting when Denis was playing'.

His fabulous talent – not only for scoring spectacular goals, but for creating them, too – allied to ferocious bravery, unquenchable enthusiasm and sheer charisma turned the club upside down. The whole atmosphere around Old Trafford changed, even though we didn't become a team of world-beaters overnight. In fact, we almost went down in his first season, 1962/63, despite his 29 goals and uplifting personal contribution. It was the winter of the big freeze, with a huge fixture backlog, and we could never build up any consistency. But occasionally we did play well, really well, revealing glimpses of what was possible, and there was an underlying feeling of excitement that we were on the verge of something special. We could see that, even though our League position was perilous at times, Matt Busby was never worried. He knew United were back on the right track, and no one played a greater part in achieving that than Denis.

I was delighted when we signed the Lawman, having experienced his fire personally during his earlier days with Manchester City. One occasion, in particular, burned itself on my memory. It was towards the end of a one-sided encounter at Old Trafford, we were leading 5-1 and Denis was smouldering at the scoreline. I was launching myself into a challenge with their centre-forward, Gerry Baker, when out of the corner of my eye I sensed a third person – and some sixth sense told me to beware. I glanced up in time to catch a fleeting glimpse of Denis, and it was clear that he wasn't coming for the ball, he was coming to do me. I just had a split second to take avoiding action, and probably that saved my career. It might have saved my life! I was a big, strong fellow, while he was only a slender lad, but I have never seen anyone more fearless, no matter what the size of his opponent. He would think nothing of diving into a melee of flying bodies to head the ball; in fact, if he could sniff a goal then he'd put his head where most people wouldn't even put their feet. Denis Law was one of the greatest players who ever lived and, certainly for his first five years at Old Trafford, before injuries began to take their toll, he exerted even more influence than did Eric Cantona some 30 years later.

Apart from his own inspirational input, he took some of the pressure off Bobby Charlton, who had experienced a couple of relatively lean seasons by his own scintillating standards. Bobby's impetus had been hindered by a hernia operation, and it's likely that he was suffering delayed reaction to the crash; whatever, the advent of Denis coincided with Charlton's resumption of his climb towards true footballing greatness.

However, despite all those positives, results continued to disappoint and in February 1963 Matt Busby spent another £53,000 on a bundle of combative creativity name of Paddy Crerand. It can't have been easy for the new arrival from Celtic to settle in a side which was striving to improve, but several early indifferent displays could not disguise the obvious fact that Paddy oozed class. He wasn't quick – in fact, he was slow – but that didn't matter in our team, which had plenty of pace in other quarters. What he supplied was guile, the ability to strike a killer pass out of nowhere. Paddy had fantastic vision, his long-range delivery was uncannily accurate and we always tried to ensure that he had plenty of space in which to operate by not requiring him to tight-mark a specific opponent.

The Crerand effect was vividly evident in the triumphant FA Cup campaign which rescued our season. Paddy slotted into midfield for the quarter-final win at Third Division Coventry City, then he helped to battle past Second Division Southampton in a dour semi-final at Villa Park, before he blossomed luxuriantly in the Wembley sunshine against Leicester City. Matt Gillies' well-organised side had enjoyed a marvellous League season, eventually finishing fourth after challenging strongly for the title at one point, and they were firm bookies' favourites against a United combination which, despite showing encouraging if fitful signs of a renaissance, had ended up fourth from the bottom of the table. On the day, though, we turned the form-book inside out, dominating the match and putting on a feast of entertaining football. Before the start I was uncharacteristically nervous, perhaps feeling an extra burden of responsibility now that I was recognised as the central bulwark of the defence. But after making an early clearance from Davie Gibson, one of the First Division's most dangerous forwards that season, I composed myself and from the moment Law put us ahead after about half an hour, I enjoyed myself enormously. The goal was a masterpiece which highlighted the particular skills of both Denis and Paddy Crerand. England goalkeeper Gordon Banks attempted to throw the ball to Gibson but Crerand, reading the action superbly, pounced to rob his fellow Scot and threaded an inch-perfect pass to Law. Denis controlled it with one assured touch, then swivelled on the spot to strike a deadly low cross-shot past Banks. After that, man-of-the-match Law was uncontrollable, wriggling past Leicester defenders seemingly at will, and it was amazing that he didn't score several more times. As it was, David Herd put us two up before Ken Keyworth pulled one back against the run of play, then David made the trophy safe at 3-1 with his second. Our team that day was David Gaskell in goal (poor Harry Gregg's season was disrupted severely by injury), Tony Dunne and skipper Noel Cantwell at full-back, a half-back line of Crerand, myself and Setters, and an all-star attack of Johnny Giles, Albert Quixall, Herd, Law and Charlton. A few more tweaks would be necessary before we returned to the Championship running – for example, a young man called George Best had yet to make his entrance – but now we knew for certain that we were on the right track.

## Ten

# Return of the glory days

**W**HAT MANNER of person was Matt Busby, the softly-spoken Scot who built one magnificent team, then another, then survived the most grievous of calamities to construct yet a third? The answer is that he was utterly remarkable, a truly great man in countless ways; although not, of course, a perfect one.

So much of the unique aura which surrounds Manchester United to this day is down to his genius. After the war he took over a hard-up club whose headquarters had been devastated by Hitler's bombs and which was run – like all clubs at that point, I would imagine – by autocratic directors accustomed to laying down the law, even in matters of football about which they knew little. Early on in his reign, Matt faced them squarely, made it clear that he would brook no interference with his work, specifying that if he did not have control then he would leave. Then, a little later, he defied the petty constraints of the domestic authorities to pioneer Britain's trail into Europe, a mammoth achievement.

Of course, that moral courage and strength of purpose, would all have counted for nothing without the expertise, the inspiration, the vision, to put together wonderful teams. He knew the game inside out, and so did his right-hand man Jimmy Murphy, on whom he leaned heavily in all day-to-day footballing matters, but above all Matt Busby was an exceptional manager of men.

He could be overwhelmingly kind, he appeared to me to have the wisdom of Solomon, he was perhaps the cleverest man I ever met, and I have never known anyone with such an imposing personal presence. He had an enormous influence on my career, guiding me steadily from my early days as the greenest of rookies, seeing something in me which perhaps others might have missed, and I owe him more than words can express.

Matt's attention to detail was legendary; nothing which could affect the wellbeing of his players, and therefore his club, was too insignificant for him. There was a time when Teresa, purely incidentally, happened to say to Jean Busby, Matt's wife, that she was not happy with the tiles in the kitchen of our club house. Lo and behold, a few days later, the manager sidled up to me and said something to the effect of: 'Bill, you really ought to be getting those tiles sorted out!' I could hardly believe my ears, but it was all good psychology, dinning into everybody associated with the club that they truly mattered. Mention of Jean, later Lady Busby, prompts me to pay a passing tribute to a truly marvellous woman. I believe that Matt, even as resilient as he was, considered giving up after Munich, but she wouldn't hear of it, knowing that he would sorely regret such a decision in the long term. That was a typical example of the wonderful support she gave her husband through the years. Lady Jean was a model for any football wife and he was never the same after her death in 1986.

To return to the man himself, he was so charming that he could cajole the birds not just from the trees, but into the palm of his hand. There are countless stories of his subtle conducting of wage negotiations. Many is the player who has gone to Matt's office, seeking a substantial pay rise, and come out delighted with a much smaller one. Similarly, if he wanted to drop you from the side, he might ask you casually how you thought you'd been playing, and more than likely you'd end up admitting, or even suggesting, that you needed a rest.

What is beyond doubt is that Matt Busby didn't wield his all-encompassing power through being a soft touch. Underneath that avuncular demeanour was a seriously ruthless character. This may surprise many people, given the public image of the two men, but the main difference between Matt Busby and Alex Ferguson is that Alex, for all his famous drive and aggression, leavens his approach with a touch of forgiveness. Matt had none whatsoever. He would not be gainsayed by anyone, and all disagreements had to end in his favour or the other party, sooner or later, would be leaving the club. In various circumstances, to which I was not privy but which could not be down to footballing problems, such marvellous players as Johnny Morris, Dennis Viollet, Johnny Giles and John Connelly all left the club.

Even Denis Law, at the peak of his powers in the mid 1960s, found that he could not brow-beat Matt Busby into giving him more money. Doubtlessly motivated by the fact that United's turnstiles were clicking merrily, he demanded a pay increase together with a signing-on fee before he would put his name to a new contract, adding the rider that if he didn't get what he wanted then he would leave Old Trafford. The manager's instant reaction was to place Denis on the transfer list, and although the two men subsequently came to an amicable arrangement, Matt had made a point to all of us in the most forceful manner possible. If he could say 'no' to Denis Law, one of the best players in the world, then what hope did the rest of us have of dictating our financial terms. Of course, he was the dominant figure at Old Trafford before that incident, but after it his power was doubled. There was a story going the rounds that Denis was told to back down in public and then be paid more money in private, but I never believed that. If I had, I would have been after him!

Perhaps it was partly due to Matt's gritty upbringing in a Scottish mining village, but he was always incredibly thrifty with the club's money. It surprised me because he was always a great family man, and he knew that players needed money to bring up their own children. A telling example of the tightness with which he controlled the pursestrings came with the lifting of the maximum wage in 1961, when Fulham instantly put Johnny Haynes on to £100 per week. We were on a mere £50. Now with all due respect to the Londoners, they were usually struggling to avoid relegation, while we were accustomed to challenging for the title and facing the cream of Europe. The times were very different then, but how we as individuals put up with that situation I don't know. Certainly today's players wouldn't, and I don't blame them. However, Matt Busby held people in the palm of his hand, and the force of his personality had to be experienced to be understood.

Come August 1963, this most charismatic of all managers was close to unleashing upon the footballing world his third and last outstanding side, but not quite all the elements were in place. This was demonstrated emphatically by the mauling we received at the hands of Everton, the League Champions, in the FA Charity Shield at Goodison Park. Matt reacted with typical decisiveness and courage, axing Giles, Quixall and Herd in favour of three youngsters, right-winger Ian Moir, inside-forward Phil Chisnall and a lanky England amateur international centre-forward named David Sadler. He gave them a run of ten-or-so games, too, as we made a reasonably successful start to the League campaign, though none of that trio was destined to make the grade in those same positions. In time Moir and Chisnall moved on to the lower divisions, while Sadler earned full England caps as a central defender, serving also as a useful midfield holding player.

Giles and Quixall departed, and an experiment with Graham Moore, a talented Welsh international inside-forward recruited from Chelsea, was not successful. But the dependable David Herd regained his place and other significant changes during the campaign saw Nobby Stiles unseat Maurice Setters and George Best claim a regular berth. The upshot was a vastly improved League position – we were runners-up to Liverpool – and a run to the semi-final of the FA Cup, where we were defeated in a Hillsborough mudbath by a Bobby Moore-inspired West Ham. That was galling, as we had now lost in two out of three successive semi-finals – Bill Nicholson's brilliant

Spurs had proved too much for us in '62, then we beat Southampton a year later – but it wasn't our most crushing disappointment of 1963/64. That came in the European Cup Winners' Cup, in which we reached the last eight by overcoming Tottenham, the holders, after being two down on the first leg. When we trounced Sporting Lisbon 4-1 in the first instalment of the quarter-final at Old Trafford, we seemed odds-on for further progress, only to be humiliated 5-0 in Portugal. I should point out, though, that there was considerable dissatisfaction in the camp during the weeks leading up to that sickening reverse. It came down to money, and once again the Boss was living up to his reputation for parsimony. When we had asked for a pay rise after winning the FA Cup, Matt Busby had upset us by playing down the achievement, saying that the cup meant comparatively little to the club, declaring that what really mattered was the Championship. In essence, the message was: win that and only then will we talk real money. That went down like a lead balloon with a group of players who were pleased and proud at having returned Manchester United to Europe, earning more money for the club in the process. That was a big deal and we felt we deserved some reward. On the pitch it seemed that everything was beginning to come together, but it wasn't being reflected in our wages. There was genuine unrest, but it amounted only to general rumblings. In retrospect we should have communicated with each other more, made a concerted effort, and then we might have achieved something. As it was, we didn't receive our bonus for winning the previous term's FA Cup until March, when we were halfway through a European quarter-final. Unbelievably the Boss didn't announce details of the package until an hour before kick-off in Lisbon. At that point, it must be said, we were delighted with the offer, but somehow the uncertainty of the situation had affected us and something happened when we walked on to that pitch. With a three-goal advantage it should have been a formality, but nothing went right, we played very poorly and we nosedived out of the competition in woefully inglorious fashion.

Overall, though, we had improved mightily by the outset of the 1964/65 season, which ended with the Championship pennant fluttering proudly from the Old Trafford flagpole for the first time since Munich. We did it with a rarely-changed side which consisted of Pat Dunne in goal, Shay Brennan and Tony Dunne (no relation) at full-back with myself and Nobby Stiles shoring up the centre of defence, Paddy Crerand and Bobby Charlton operating as a supremely skilful play-making unit in midfield, John Connelly on the right wing, Denis Law and David Herd up front, with number-11 George Best nominally on the left flank, but actually roaming to every corner of the pitch.

At this point a word or two of introduction to some players is in order, while further appeciation of others would not come amiss. With Harry Gregg and David Gaskell both being plagued by injury, the manager drafted in the affable Dubliner Pat Dunne between the posts, and he served us nobly throughout a memorable campaign. Pat was not world-class, it would be idle to pretend otherwise, but he was a marvellous shot-stopper and unfailingly brave. Certainly, he didn't let us down, remaining ever-present after making his debut in September in a 3-3 draw at Everton, ironically a club he had served as a junior.

Shay Brennan was a pleasure to play alongside, a delight to be with both on and off the field. He was terrific under the most severe pressure, nothing seemed to faze him. As a former wing-half and inside-forward, it's not surprising that he was endowed with lovely ball control and could pass beautifully, but also he had this instinctive positional sense which frequently rescued us from trouble. He was not a thunderous tackler but he had a knack of jockeying opponents away from goal, guiding them subtly out of the immediate danger area. Shay was a fantastic asset to the dressing room, too, an absolute charmer. He was great mates with Bobby and Nobby, and when Bobby was in serious mode, if anyone could get him to laugh then it was Shay.

Tony Dunne was one of the unsung heroes of the British game, a hugely underrated performer where press and public were concerned, but his team-mates appreciated him to the hilt. He was unbelievably quick, so that even if he happened to lose a tackle, invariably he would recover in time to have another bite at his opponent. He was like an insurance policy for the rest of us, too; we knew there was always hope with Tony around. Importantly, he would never take risks with the ball, invariably opting for a sensible pass to one of the midfielders, but he could play a bit, as he proved when he assumed more responsibility late in his career with Bolton Wanderers. He had arrived unheralded, a bargain buy from Shelbourne in the Republic of Ireland in the spring of 1960, after which he demonstrated his mettle by ousting, in time, no less a rival than club captain Noel Cantwell.

One player who really blossomed in 1964/65 was Nobby Stiles. I had a reputation for toughness but I don't know where it came from because it was Nobby who was doing most of the kicking. Usually I'd be intercepting or heading the ball, making use of my size and power but not making that many tackles. Meanwhile Nobby was getting stuck in, putting in all the ground-level challenges. As tenacious as a terrier with the courage of a lion, he threw himself into everything and picked up loads of bookings, while I received only one in my entire career. I like to think that we complemented one another, that my experience helped Nobby while his constant frenetic involvement, as well as his intelligent reading of the action, was of immeasurable benefit to me. One of our rules was never to speak to opponents. Some liked to chat on the pitch but we would have none of that because it is all too easy to have your concentration shattered which, of course, was exactly what they wanted.

Two Scottish internationals, Paddy Crerand and David Herd, both rose to new heights during this title season, Paddy combining ever more sweetly with Bobby in the centre of the park, and David scoring freely while offering fabulous support to our world-class triumvirate of Charlton, Law and Best with his selfless industry, much of it off the ball.

Another player who did not always collect the accolades he deserved was right-winger John Connelly, a canny £56,000 signing from Burnley in April 1964 and a St Helens lad like myself. An established England international, John was already a title-winner, having played a major part in the Turf Moor club's triumph of 1959/60, and he proved to be a catalyst of United's success. Quick, direct and willing to chase back in the manner of a modern midfielder, John contributed plenty of goals, passed beautifully and offered perfect balance to the more intricate skills of George, who began each game on the opposite flank. It was a shame that John left as early as 1966, when he had several more good years in him, following a disagreement with the Boss.

And so, as ever when the mid-1960s team is under discussion, to that incomparable trinity of Charlton, Law and Best. It is my sincere belief that never in England, in Britain, perhaps even in Europe have three such brilliant footballers served the same side, and that includes even Real Madrid and Honved, the sumptuous Hungarian team of the 1950s. Bobby, about whom I have already waxed lyrical, attained his regal pomp when withdrawn from the left wing, where he had spent the early part of the decade, to central midfield, his passing and vision majestic, his stamina exceptional and his shooting as spectacular as ever.

Law? He was a paragon, both a sensational individual and a superb team man. Whereas Bobby loved to run with the ball, Denis rarely dribbled, although he had the ability to do so, in fact he could do anything. He was all about quicksilver movement, electric one-touch magic and a burning desire to win which occasionally landed him in trouble with referees. Matt had problems with his fellow Scot's bursts of indiscpline during games, but knew it was all part of the irresistible cocktail of attributes which made him a special player. Thus the manager was willing to accept the situation. It became a standing joke with the other players that Denis would be sent off three times in the first half of the season, so that he would be suspended in time to be home in Aberdeen in time for Christmas! Of course, it was the grossest of exaggerations, but that's how dressing-room banter goes.

Off the field, there were no difficulties with Law, who was an exemplary professional. I was never a close friend of his because I was a bit of a loner, but so was he in his own particular way. Oh, he loved the crack with the other players, and had a laugh, and was extremely popular. He could light the place up with his bright and breezy manner, even if some of his jokes tended to be on the sarcastic side. But I always felt that this extrovert aspect of his personality went only so far, that deep down he was always a very private man with hidden depths. In that respect, perhaps, he was a Jekyll and Hyde character.

Now I've mentioned ten members of our 1964/65 title-winning combination, which brings me to the eleventh, and the most amazing of them all – George Best. Harry Gregg was training with me at the Cliff one day when he said there was a little guy at the club whom he'd never seen the like of before. Apparently he cut a frail figure, was little more than a wisp of a lad, but he was strong on the ball and his dribbling skills were utterly dazzling. Quite simply, said Harry, he was the most phenomenal thing he had ever seen on a football field. At the time I thought our eloquent Irish goalkeeper was going over the top, as he was prone to do on occasion, but this time he was 100 per cent correct. In my opinion, George Best was the most astonishing raw talent the game has ever known. Yes, I'd put him up there with Pele, Maradona, di Stefano, Cruyff, or anyone else under the sun. We felt we had the makings of a top team already, but then George appeared and kicked us into a new dimension. His footballing make-up was practically flawless and I believe he could have excelled in any position. Everyone knows about his unbelievable all-round skill, destructive speed and sinewy athleticism, but it is not always appreciated how tough he was. George could tackle like a full-back, he was as strong as any opponent I've ever met, and he was so, so brave, as he had to be to ride some of the outrageous challenges which he faced in match after match. True, there were times when he held the ball so long that he infuriated other members of the team, but more often than not, just as they were about to complain, he would stick the ball in the net from a seemingly impossible position. Then there was the fact, which nobody admitted, that when George was dribbling on his merry way, the rest of us could take a bit of a breather!

So it was with such unparalleled quality that Manchester United went into the 1964/65 campaign, which threw up one of the most exciting Championship races of all time, with Don Revie's emerging Leeds and Tommy Docherty's precocious Chelsea sides offering the principal opposition. We started pretty well but then hit an indifferent patch around mid-term before coming back strongly when it mattered the most. We were chasing honours on three fronts and when we lost a bitterly contested FA Cup semi-final replay to Leeds – Billy Bremner grabbed a late winner after we had dominated most of the action – many critics wrote us off. That made us all the more determined, particularly when we went to Elland Road in mid April for what was billed widely as a potential title decider. On a blustery, raw day which made flowing football virtually impossible, we battled to a 1-0 victory, and our hero was John Connelly. Not only did he score the crucial goal, but he never stopped running, harassing Bobby Collins ceaselessly, reducing the combatively influential little schemer's effectiveness virtually to nil.

That gave us an advantage which we never relinquished, and we claimed the crown in the penultimate game, a 3-1 home win over Arsenal. I knew that we would be okay provided we won and Leeds didn't, and when we went two goals up, news filtered through that the Yorkshiremen were trailing by three at Birmingham. At that moment I shook hands with Shay Brennan and asked him what it was like to win his first Championship medal. It was unprofessional of me – uncharacteristic, too, I like to think – and this was brought home to me forcefully as George Eastham pulled one back for the Gunners, then we heard that Leeds had recovered to 3-3 at St Andrew's. Happily, we steadied the ship to take both points, after which it would have needed a 17-0 reverse in our final game at Aston Villa for Leeds to pip us. In the event we lost 2-1, but there was never the remotest danger of a slip-up on the scale required, and we ended up as Champions on goal average.

Quite properly, our free-scoring forwards were accorded lavish adulation for their part in the achievement and, it's true, they were magnificent. All five reached double figures – Law 28, Herd 20, Connelly 15, Charlton and Best 10 each – but I feel the defence deserved a word or two of praise, too, particularly for our record when the pressure was on near the end. There was a crucial sequence of five clean sheets in the space of six games, which gave our front-men a solid base from which to create their magic. All in all it was a wonderful team effort and, enjoyable though the 1963 FA Cup triumph had been, it was only now that we believed Manchester United had truly been reborn as a major force.

At that point we were still in Europe, having reached the semi-finals of the old Inter-Cities Fairs Cup (now renamed the UEFA Cup), and because of our crowded fixture list, the authorities bent their rules to allow us to play those matches in June, way after the season's normal closing date. In the last four we faced Ferencvaros of Hungary, which for Bobby Charlton and myself meant our first return behind the Iron Curtain since the air crash. It was a harrowing experience, particularly when we drew after two legs and needed a play-off in Budapest to conclude matters. By then it was high summer and we were jaded, and despite having the better of the tie over the three games, we bowed out 5-4 on aggregate, having missed a host of scoring chances. Our dream of carrying off a European trophy would have to wait, but another opportunity would not be long in coming.

In fact, it seemed that no sooner had we completed our obligations in Hungary than the new season was beginning, which highlighted a particular problem with United in the 1960s. Although we had a very fine team, a great one even, we never had sufficient depth of squad as we had, say, before the crash. That meant that almost every season, come the spring, perhaps half the team were playing on when they were almost crippled with niggling injuries. As a result we experienced collective burn-out, mental as well as physical if the truth be told, and although we did not go short of silverware exactly, we didn't achieve all that we might have done had we had a few more top-quality players to bring in. Certainly Law and Best played far too many times when they were in serious discomfort. I played in pain regularly, and frequently I was carrying an injury which limited my effectiveness. How I would have relished the occasional couple of weeks' rest, perhaps supplemented by a bit of light training. That's what happens in these modern days of squad rotation; if a top player is hurt then another top player comes in, and it plays an important part in maintaining optimum fitness levels. The culture was different in the 1960s, when you always turned out your first-choice line-up if it was humanly possible, no matter what. I'm not trying to make excuses, but I believe the old short-sighted regime was a major factor in United's rotten record in semi-finals during that decade. We bowed out in the last four of the FA Cup in 1962 to Spurs, 1964 to West Ham, 1965 to Leeds and 1966 to Everton; in addition, we fell to Ferencvaros in the Fairs Cup of 1965 and, as we shall see, to Partizan in the European Cup of 1966. We won through in the FA Cup in 1963 and the European Cup in 1968, but for a team of United's class I don't believe that six defeats to two victories is an acceptable ratio. Equally I don't believe it was due to lack of footballing ability or mental strength, so I return to the lack of an adequate squad.

This was especially galling in 1965/66 when a frankly poor early run made it highly unlikely that we were going to retain our League crown. This culminated in a 5-1 annihilation by Tottenham at White Hart Lane in October, when Jimmy Greaves scored one of his most celebrated goals. He picked up the ball in midfield and, seemingly never rising above a casual pace, he waltzed past four tackles – I was one of the victims, being tricked by his sublime dummy – before tucking his shot neatly past Pat Dunne. In truth, there was no shame in that. I rate Jimmy as the finest specialist finisher I have ever seen. A couple of months later we gained our revenge, reversing the scoreline in an Old Trafford mudbath, a hugely satisfying win which featured a Bobby Charlton rasper which was special even by his exalted standards. However, that was by no means enough to lift us into title contention, so even more attention than usual was focused on the knockout competitions. In the FA Cup we progressed past Derby County (comfortably) and Rotherham (shakily) before encountering Wolves at Molineux in the fifth round, which shaped up in the opening minutes as a personal nightmare. Twice I attempted to control the ball on my chest, twice I failed, twice my hand shot out in a reflex action, and twice the referee gave penalties. Terry Wharton converted both and, understandably enough, my team-mates were glaring at me as if I was out of my mind. At half-time Matt was brilliant, just telling me to forget about it, but I was devastated that I had got us into such a mess. But then Denis Law came to my rescue, scoring two goals as we took control to finish 4-2 winners, and one of his strikes when he appeared to hover in mid-air before netting at the far post, was out of this world. It was around the time of his rumbling pay dispute and as Wolves kicked off after that goal, one of their players remarked to Denis: 'If I could do that I'd play this f****** game for nothing.' The Lawman's reply was typically succinct: 'I do!' he said. After such a stirring comeback it was a crying shame that we should bow out to a single goal by Everton's Colin Harvey in the semi-final, a match which followed hard on the heels of two immensely taxing European games.

That season I really believed we could win the European Cup. Despite our disappointing First Division form, our side was perfectly balanced, and although I celebrated ny 34th birthday that January, I had never felt fitter. Several years of experience at centre-half was standing me in good stead and I was strolling through the games, relishing every moment of it. Early indications could hardly have been more positive as we disposed of HJK Helsinki 9-2 on aggregate, then overcame ASK Vorwarts 5-1, although not before an unexpected disruption shortly before the first leg. As we went through the American checkpoint into East Berlin we had to fill out forms and Paddy Crerand gave his name and number as James Bond 007. The border officials did not think it was very funny at all and they held us there for three hours, which was hardly ideal preparation for a game the next day. It's a long time ago now, but I seem to recall that Paddy had the good grace to look a tad embarrassed. As it turned out, the delay didn't faze us and we returned home from Eastern Europe with a 2-0 win, a rare achievement garnished by David Herd's hat-trick in the second leg.

That took us through to the quarter-finals where we were paired with mighty Benfica of Portugal, one of the great names of European soccer. We were not overawed, however, and in the first leg at Old Trafford Nobby imposed his authority on the brilliant Eusebio. Still Benfica scored first, but when I headed one of my rare goals it put us 3-1 up, only for the Eagles to pull one back at the death. Suddenly all our mounting elation drained away; with only a single goal advantage to take with us to the Stadium of Light, there was sharp doubt that we would win through.

Matt reacted in a way which was rare for him – he laid special defensive plans for the away leg. Normally he would tell us to seize the initiative early on, get in front and then simply score as many as possible, but this time he preached caution, instructing us to get everyone but David Herd behind the ball for the first 20 minutes, to funnel back as far as was necessary to frustrate our opponents, and to attack only on the break. With Benfica clearly convinced that we would go for their throats as usual, the strategy worked a treat. Playing so deep, George had never been given as much space in his life and he was rampant, scoring two scintillating goals and looking world-class as Connelly, Charlton and Crerand added further strikes in our 5-1 victory on the night. Quite rightly, George monopilised the headlines the next day – he was christened 'El Beatle' when he arrived back in England sporting a sombrero, and life was never quite the same again for soccer's first pop-star – but I must say a word about the performance of Harry Gregg. Benfica's towering centre-forward, Jose Torres, was fantastic in the air so it was decided that while I should cover everything which came up the middle, Harry should come out for every cross, hoping to catch the ball but at least doing his best to distract the Portuguese beanpole. Essentially that was Harry's game anyway, and he played his part magnificently, spending much of his time airborne but also frequently hurling himself fearlessly at forwards' feet. United's other goalkeepers of the 1960s – David Gaskell, Pat Dunne and Alex Stepney – all won major medals, and it was a travesty that Harry, arguably the best of them all, should eventually leave Old Trafford without a club gong to his name. But for a debilitating sequence of injuries, I'm certain that he would have been weighed down with the honours he so richly deserved. Still, at least he had played his part in arguably the greatest ever performance by an English team on foreign soil, the thrashing of Europe's top team in front of their own fans.

After that, United were red-hot favourites to lift the trophy, but what awaited us was the direst of anti-climaxes, defeat at the hands of unfancied Partizan Belgrade. We made things difficult for ourselves by losing 2-0 in Yugoslavia, though our forwards, most uncharacteristically, missed a hatful of comparatively easy chances. We were sorely handicapped by taking the field with several players – Best, Law and myself – far from fit, and by the end poor George was no more than a limping passenger. In the second leg we battered them and Nobby managed one goal, but we should have scored another five and, although we felt we had precious little help from the referee, we had only ourselves to blame for not taking our opportunities. It was a colossal disappointment because we knew we'd had an excellent chance of winning the European Cup and we had blown it. We all felt we had failed Matt, the fans and the club. What made it worse was that we believed the team had peaked, and that it might have been our last chance. Happily, fate had something more memorable in store.

Certainly, we went into 1966/67 burning with the desire to erase memories of recent under-achievement, but we didn't get the start we craved. At times we played brilliantly and racked up the goals, but at others we were poor, and Matt Busby was forced to make changes.

The most significant of these, perhaps, was the arrival of goalkeeper Alex Stepney from Chelsea, who did exceptionally well, especially when you consider that he had played only one First Division game for his former club. Before that his only League experience had been with Millwall in the lower regions. Others to make a major impact were the admirably versatile David Sadler, who had spells up front and at the back, and young John Aston, a gritty, industrious winger whose father had featured in Matt Busby's first fine team and was now an Old Trafford coach. But the newcomer who appeared to have the brightest future was a flinty young Mancunian named Bobby Noble, who was called up after we had suffered a thrashing by Nottingham Forest at the City Ground. Bobby operated at left-back, with Tony Dunne moving to the right and Shay losing his place, but he played with the polish of any midfielder. His reading of the game was immaculate, his control and distribution were of the highest order, he was tough as teak and as quick as a whippet. I could see nothing standing between Bobby Noble and an illustrious future as an England international, but towards the end of the season he suffered terrible injuries in a car accident and never played again, despite harrowing attempts at a comeback in training. That was a tremendous blow to United, just when we needed a new generation of defenders, and a personal tragedy for the lad.

Back in the autumn I had passed a personal milestone at White Hart Lane, when I became the first man to play 500 League games for the club, though I was hardly in the mood to celebrate in view of a 2-1 defeat. Soon afterwards my fortunes took a dip when I was sidelined by a calf injury and questions were raised about the long-term future of this particular thirtysomething. However, I found myself back in the side on Boxing Day, when we lost to Sheffield United at Bramall Lane. Happily that proved to be our last reverse of the campaign as we embarked on a glorious sequence of winning our home games and drawing on our travels, the classic recipe for lifting titles. Early in the New Year it looked as if our main rivals would be Liverpool, the reigning champs, and Johnny Carey's Forest, but Bill

Shankly's men fell away rather surprisingly and we were left to battle for supremacy with the fine Nottingham side, guided so enter-prisingly by our former skipper.

Without any European distraction this time around, and having been evicted unceremoniously from the FA Cup by Second Division Norwich City, we had more recovery time between League matches, and in the end we triumphed with a game to spare. The issue was decided on an unforgettable afternoon at West Ham, where we romped home 6-1, and I even managed to score a goal. We had a corner and I made a late run into the box, took the ball on my chest and volleyed into the corner of the net with my right foot, an untypical example of my deadly finishing which put us three up just before the interval. The second half was obviously enjoyable, but there was no way I was going to relax, and some time before the end when Nobby congratulated me on winning my fourth title medal, I swore at him and told him to get on with the game. It was a conversation that we had a laugh about afterwards, although he has never allowed me to forget it!

When it was all over I looked back on the campaign with considerable satisfaction, but also with a tinge of regret. I was delighted to have collected another gong, to have played in front of massive crowds week in and week out, and to have contributed four goals, one of which secured a draw at Maine Road. Beyond any doubt I was relishing the happiest playing period of my career. I was entrenched in the centre-half role that I loved, I was making my living with a wonderful bunch of guys, and certainly it was both a pleasure and a privilege to line up alongside the likes of George Best, Denis Law and Bobby Charlton. But hovering over it all, for me at any rate, there was a nagging feeling that we had some unfinished business on the European front. With my 36th birthday due to fall in 1967/68, and with other members of the side also getting rather long in the tooth, was there still time to complete it?

# Eleven

# Rainbow's end

I WAS SO fortunate with injuries, steering clear of serious problems throughout most of my career. But one afternoon around New Year in 1968 my luck ran out. I wasn't due to work that day but I had become interested in coaching and decided to visit the gym at our training ground, The Cliff, to watch the youngsters go through their paces. So I was utterly relaxed, in my civvies and with my attention momentarily directed elsewhere, when two of the lads, Carlo Sartori and Brian Kidd, got into a good-natured scuffle. Apparently Carlo gave Brian a shove and he fell across my leg, which happened to be outstretched. There was a horrible sound of something tearing and it turned out to be my cruciate ligament. After all those years of playing at the top club level, it seemed that my career might have been ended by a freak accident. There was not one jot of malice involved, and I didn't hold anything against the two boys, even though it seemed likely that they had finished me. After all, I was almost 36 and in those days even players who were 15 years younger didn't often come back from torn cruciates. I was rushed into the treatment room and put straight into splints before being driven home by our trainer, Jack Crompton. When Teresa opened the door she couldn't believe her eyes, she thought we were pulling some practical joke as she knew I had not been playing that day. I wished!

It was a shattering blow, not least because I had been enjoying myself so much during the first part of the season, and United had been doing so well, riding high at the top of the table despite the periodic loss to injury of such key contributors as Denis Law and Nobby Stiles. I was in my element, barely breaking sweat but feeling more in control than at any time since I had arrived at Old Trafford.

Now the picture changed dramatically. The side began to lose matches it might have expected to win and earlier indications that we might retain our title with some degree of comfort took a nosedive. Almost immediately we bowed out of the FA Cup, being beaten by Spurs after a replay, and our prospects in the European Cup began to look considerably more daunting. Thus far we had progressed to the quarter-finals at the expense of Hibernians of Malta (4-0 on aggregate) and Sarajevo (a much tighter tie, which we had shaded 2-1), and now faced tough and skilful opposition in the form of Gornik Zabrze, the famous mining-town club.

After a couple of months, although I was still in plenty of pain, I began to train after a fashion and Matt encouraged a speedy return to action. He told me I looked great, but I knew I wasn't, and I wasn't anywhere near making the first leg against Gornik, which we won 2-0 at Old Trafford on February 28. Still, I went over to Poland for the return encounter and the manager exerted further pressure on me to play. But the pitch was a sheet of ice, made even more treacherous by a covering of snow, and I knew that I could be no more than a passenger. So I ruled myself out and he didn't take it well, not even speaking to me for a couple of weeks afterwards. In the event David Sadler excelled at centre-half, doing a brilliant job of marking the outstanding Wlodzimierz Lubanski and, with Nobby Stiles, Tony Dunne, young Francis Burns and John Fitzpatrick all contributing magnificently to a lengthy rearguard action, we squeezed through on aggregate, losing only 1-0 on the night, which was quite an achievement in front of 105,000 partisan Polish supporters. In my state there was no way I could have equalled David's performance but, given Matt's attitude, my evening on the bench was chilly in more ways than one. After Gornik I continued to train, but despite making some progress my knee blew up and fluid needed to be aspirated from it after every session, so I missed the next half-dozen League games, a period during which our Championship hopes took a further buffeting. All the while Nobby and Denis were turning out pretty regularly, despite not being fully fit, and basically it was the old story of United not being able to give a decent account of themselves in the spring because of inadequate squad resources. Eventually I was pitched back into the First Division fray on Easter Saturday, when we drew 2-2 with Southampton, then appeared again just two days later in a 3-0 win over Fulham. Inevitably, though, I broke down once more, which meant that I would be absent for the first leg of the European Cup semi-final against our old rivals, the mighty Real Madrid, at Old Trafford. That night the Stretford Enders were at their most wildly vociferous as United poured forward relentlessly, pressing the Spanish aristocrats constantly and creating a succession of scoring opportunities; but at the end of a passionate contest, all we had to show for our efforts was a 1-0 lead, courtesy of a bullet-shot from George Best ten minutes before the break.

The general consensus of opinion was that we needed a far more decisive advantage to take into the second leg in Spain three weeks hence, but there was no time to dwell on might-have-beens, as we were still embroiled in a race for the title with Manchester City. Despite recent lapses, we remained the favourites, but alas we slipped badly, and a 2-1 home defeat by Sunderland on the final day – during which I had to be taken off when my knee seized up – confirmed our fate. All credit to Joe Mercer's side, which contained the likes of Colin Bell, Francis Lee and Mike Summerbee. They were an exceptionally fine team and I would never dispute that they were worthy Champions, but I felt in my heart that we should, and would, have retained our crown, but for our injury situation.

Still, there was a European Cup semi-final to look forward to and, after monitoring me closely in training, Matt decreed that I should play. On one hand I was delighted to be involved, but on the other

I was almost sick with apprehension, so desperate was I not to let the team, the manager and the fans down. He understood my worries, told me I'd get through with Nobby and Tony covering for me, and in the end he was right. However, even Matt could not have anticipated the scale of the ordeal which faced us in that seething Bernabeu cauldron. At first Real Madrid were all over us and although Alex Stepney made a series of brilliant saves, they scored three times in the first half through the perceptive Pirri, the evergreen veteran Gento – my tormentor of old – and Amancio, who was a constant menace. In return all we could muster was a single strike, and that was courtesy of an own-goal, a chronic miskick from Zoco. We were playing badly and things looked pretty bleak, but in the dressing room Matt Busby pulled a master-stroke. He reminded us that we were only 3-2 down on aggregate and that there was still a real chance for us. That lifted a few heads, gave us a fresh perspective, and then Real Madrid played straight into our hands. They thought they had it won and began show-boating, playing keep-ball long before it was safe. We battled on, all the time remembering Matt's words at the interval, and when David Sadler, who was operating effectively in midfield, nudged in a goal 20 minutes from the end, Real just couldn't believe it. They seemed to freeze, as if a prize had been snatched from their grasp, and that encouraged us to attack.

But what happened next was the stuff of sheer fantasy; in fact, I don't think I could have dreamed it. United got a throw-in on halfway and, although I was not in the habit of piling forward, now something prompted me to advance. I said to Nobby Stiles, who was far more likely than me to get in the opposition's half: 'Stay here, I'm going up.' He asked me what the hell I was doing, but I didn't hang around for a debate. I showed for the ball but Paddy Crerand, doubtlessly unable to believe his own eyes, threw it to George Best. Now George went down the right touchline, dancing past several tackles, and I kept going, too. Eventually, when he looked up, I was the only United player in the box. My first thought was that he would never pass to me and that he would try to score at the near post. But as he feinted one way, wrong-footing the defenders, I read what was in his mind. I had seen him do it so often, albeit with Denis or Bobby or David in the middle instead of me. So I took three steps back and, sure enough, he rolled it into my path. All I had to do was sidefoot it into the net. It all seemed unreal, like I was frozen in time. When everyone came to congratulate me the first thing I did was to tell Nobby to stay back because there were still 15 minutes to go. He said: 'You miserable bugger!' and clearly George wondered why I wasn't showing any emotion. But I saved that for later. All that mattered to me then was that, having yanked ourselves back into command, we didn't let it all slip away. I needn't have worried. Real Madrid appeared to be in a state of stupor, utterly stunned by the turnaround, enabling us to finish in comfortable control. Over the years since, I have had plenty of praise for that goal, but I'd like to place on record my indebtedness to the men who did so much to get me through the game, my defensive comrades, particularly Nobby and Tony. I have never known two men better at covering a big centre-half such as myself, and rarely did they play more superbly than they did on that memorable evening at the Bernabeu.

Afterwards, of course, there was euphoria in the United camp. Matt asked me what on earth I had been doing in Real's penalty area, and I could offer no rational explanation, but neither of us cared about that. It was very emotional, the feeling that we had reached the final ten years on from Munich, but this was no time for relaxation. Happily, after the game I felt strong and my knee felt good, in sharp contrast to my condition during the Sunderland debacle. Still, I was taking nothing for granted and it was an almighty relief to me when, on the way home, the Boss said to me quietly: 'Get yourself ready for the final. You've got two weeks with no games. I believe you can do it.' So he'd more or less told me that I would be playing against Benfica at Wembley, and that gave me so much confidence. Over the next ten days or so I practically killed myself in training, I had never worked so hard in my life. Weights, running alone, long distance and short, I went through the lot, inspired through every moment by the thought that I was on the threshold of the pinnacle of my career. This is what everything had been building up to. True I had a few anxious moments when my knee ballooned, but each time I went to the doctor and had it aspirated, then got back to my rigorous regime. Three days before the final I stopped, just contented myself with hitting a few golf balls on the practice range, and strolled around the gardens of our lovely hotel near Windsor, where Matt had taken us to prepare for the match of a lifetime. What must have been going through his mind, I cannot begin to speculate, what with all the toil and triumph and tragedy of the previous ten years. Of course, he had to remain level-headed, to name the right team to take on the talented Portuguese, who remained a daunting combination despite having slipped a little since their peak of a couple of seasons earlier. A little like United, you could say.

In the end, with poor Denis Law practically demented at having to miss out because of a knee operation, the Boss had one difficult decision to make, whether to name rookie Francis Burns or the experienced Shay Brennan as full-back partner to Tony Dunne. Throughout most of the campaign Francis had been the man in possession, missing only one European match until Matt opted for the wily Shay to combat Francisco Gento in the second meeting with Real Madrid. So well had the Irish international performed that the manager opted to stick with him, which must have been devastating for the youngster, but he took it well. Thus we lined-up as follows: Alex Stepney in goal, a back line of Shay Brennan, myself, Nobby Stiles and Tony Dunne, Paddy Crerand and Bobby Charlton as central creators with David Sadler buzzing around in a holding role, George Best and John Aston on the flanks, and Brian Kidd at the front, spearheading the attack on his 19th birthday.

Now I have played in an awful lot of games, but never before or afterwards did I experience the particular feeling I had as we walked out at Wembley, resplendent in our change-strip of all-blue. In the dressing room I had been a bit edgy, thinking that we were a team essentially on the way down, that we would need a truly Herculean effort to take the European Cup. But as we moved through the tunnel and on to the pitch, and the crowd erupted all around us, I felt an incredible sensation of uplift. It was almost spiritual, and maybe was something to do with the long and tortuous path taken by Manchester United to reach this point in history. Certainly it left no room for doubt. Suddenly I felt charged with belief in myself and my team-mates, I didn't even contemplate the possibility of defeat. This was absolute pleasure, and it couldn't have happened on a more appropriate occasion. I reflected that I had no way of knowing if the feeling was personal to me, but that if it was common to all of us, then we would be unbeatable.

Of course, we had to be careful. It was a balmy, stiflingly hot night so energy would be at a premium, and Benfica remained a potent force; certainly in their panther-like inside-forward, Eusebio, they boasted one of the greatest footballers of all time, a fellow who could turn any contest with one flash of inspiration. He gave us an early reminder of his class, too, cracking the bar with a fabulous swerving shot from 30 yards, but in general Nobby – who was carrying an injury but hid the fact brilliantly – policed him to terrific effect. That one torrid moment apart, Manchester United dominated the first half, driving forward time after time, only to miss our chances. Two or three of them fell to David Sadler, who was working his heart out but appeared just a little over-anxious in front of goal, rather snatching at the ball instead of taking his time. Meanwhile John Aston was having the match of his life on the left wing. Most of the time he was marked by only one defender and if John went by that man, which he did repeatedly, then he had the whole field to run into. Once he got going they had no way of stopping him and he tore them to shreds. In stark contrast, on the opposite flank George Best was always surrounded by a posse of opponents, which was frustrating for the Irishman – who displayed the occasional flicker of petulance as a result – but merely created more space for John.

At half-time we didn't need lifting; it felt obvious to us that if we carried on in the same vein then we were bound to score sooner or later, and so it proved after 53 minutes. It was appropriate that the provider was David Sadler, who drifted a curving cross from the left and the ball slid off the top of Bobby's head at the near post, beating goalkeeper Henrique at the far upright. I'm not sure if Bob made the contact he wanted but it didn't matter – we had the lead we deserved, and at that point I thought the game was wrapped up. Paddy, David and Bobby were getting through a staggering amount of work in midfield – I had never seen Paddy play better – while Nobby appeared to have Eusebio pretty well in his pocket; Shay and Tony were covering immaculately, John and George were frightening their markers to death and Brian Kidd was roaming dangerously, pulling their defenders all over the place. As for me, I felt I had managed to do my job, which was to keep the giant Jose Torres under wraps. He was a supremely awkward customer, about four inches taller than me and wirily strong. Celtic boss Jock Stein, in praising our semi-final victory, had warned about the aerial threat of the Portuguese centre-forward, stressing that Benfica channelled everything through him and that if he could be suppressed then they were only half the team. As well as scoring goals himself, he had a knack of gliding the ball with his forehead to the feet of Eusebio or Mario Coluna, and he had honed it to a fine art. But I had my own method against him, one I had evolved over the years in battles with big rangy opponents such as Andy Lochhead of Burnley and Keith Ellis of Sheffield Wednesday. It involved using the striker's body to lever myself into the air and, okay, technically it was illegal. However, not for a second do I believe it was immoral. I felt I was just using my own god-given abilities, pitting them against his. I might not have been the world's most delicate manipulator of a ball, but I thought I was a good defender, and this was an integral part of my craft. It was all a matter of timing. When a high ball came in, I would concentrate on his movement and aim to leap a split second before him, often using his calves as a launching pad. I'd found that if I disguised the contact carefully it was almost impossible for a referee to detect, and as a result it was extremely rare for me to give away free-kicks in dangerous positions, which Matt saw as a huge plus. Naturally Torres didn't like it, and he spent a fair part of the evening complaining to referee Concetto Lo Bello. Once he pointed to rake-marks down the back of his legs but it was nothing serious; the Italian official waved him away with a sweeping gesture and the big fellow looked crestfallen, then gave me the blackest look imaginable. I didn't respond, merely redoubling my concentration, and as the match wore on I didn't allow him any headers except a couple well outside the danger area. But we were unable to add to our lead despite having the majority of the play and, with only 11 minutes remaining, finally Torres won the ball where it mattered, nodding a flighted delivery from Jose Augusto into the path of Graca, who netted with a fierce, low cross-shot. I thought: 'Christ, he's done it. If they get another one we've had it,' but then I banished it from my mind and resumed my concentration. Still, though, there was a moment of pure nightmare in store. With only three minutes to go, Eusebio burst through the middle and went past Nobby; I was caught a bit wide and for once even Tony wasn't there, so we had no cover. I couldn't believe it as we were so well organised, but in that mortifying instant there was nothing else to do but to give chase. I wasn't gaining on him, Nobby was though not quickly enough, but I'm sure Eusebio must have heard the thunder of pursuit as we bore down on him, one on either side. Whatever, he had to hurry, and in the crucial split-second he made the wrong decision. If he'd opted to place the ball clinically then Alex Stepney would not have stood a chance, but in that blurred moment in which the Portuguese star shaped to blast it, somehow I felt we would be all right. Then the ball thudded into Alex's midriff, and he held on beautifully, leaving Eusebio utterly dumbfounded. I think he felt so guilty at having squandered his golden chance that he ran on and congratulated our 'keeper for his effort, as if to say it was a good save rather than a bad shot. In the heat of battle, Alex was having none of it, rejecting the great man's advances almost curtly as if to say: 'Piss off, we've got a game on, no time for niceties!' which was typical of Stepney's professionalism.

Undoubtedly that was the turning point of the game, the moment in which it died for Benfica. Shortly afterwards the whistle went for the end of normal time and Matt Busby's job was easy. He told us to look at the body-language of the Portuguese, who were sagging. The Boss said: 'They are beaten. Just go and finish the job.' And we did so, quickly and emphatically, with three goals in the first ten minutes of added time. First Kiddo glanced on a Stepney clearance to Best, who had switched to the left flank; George nipped beyond Jacinto, then rounded goalkeeper Henrique before rolling the ball almost gently into the Benfica net. It was a fabulous goal from a stupendous player, although later Shay Brennan claimed the credit because he had started the move with a back-pass to Alex! Now United poured forward non-stop and birthday-boy Brian headed the third at the second attempt after Sadler had turned a Charlton corner-kick across goal, then the young southpaw from Collyhurst sprinted down the right and crossed with his unfavoured foot for Bobby to clip home the fourth at the near post. By now Wembley was rocking, it was absolute bedlam. As Kenneth Wolstenholme pointed out in his commentary, the United fans were outshouting even the England supporters who had cheered Alf Ramsey's team to World Cup victory two years earlier. I suppose there wasn't much meaningful football played in the second half of extra-time, but it ranks as the most enjoyable interlude of my career. To know we had won the most coveted prize of all, yet still be able to play on in front of our delirious followers, gave me the most fantastic feeling.

It wasn't until some time after the match that I was struck by the massive scale of our achievement, but even as the final whistle went I could see that Bobby was overwhelmed. We had been through a lot together, but now we just looked at each other and words were not necessary. He sank to his knees and he was crying, utterly drained not only by the incredible physical effort he had put in – I don't know where he found the energy to run non-stop for two hours on such a sweltering evening – but also, perhaps, by deep emotions concerning the lads who lost their lives while questing for the European Cup. There was no way I was going to interfere with his thoughts at a time like that and, in the circumstances, I was not surprised that he was unable to attend the banquet that night. Much later we had a joke about the game, with Bobby telling me I hadn't really been needed after all! When you know him well he's got a great sense of humour, no matter what outsiders might think.

Meanwhile, in contrast, Matt was not delaying the expression of his joy, which was clearly overwhelming. He gave me a giant hug but, like Bobby, he didn't say anything, even though we had come the whole way together to become Champions of Europe and that finally we had managed the only fitting tribute to the victims of Munich. Those were different days, when celebrations were far more restrained. People go mad today, they carry it on forever even for the scoring of a routine goal. In my view that's completely over the top.

This party, of course, was anything but routine and the lads had a great time. I have rarely seen a bigger grin than the one which split the face of David Sadler, normally such a serious lad, and had he been just a little more composed with his finishing it might have been plastered all over the front pages of the newspapers the next day. After all, he might have scored a hat-trick, emulating Geoff Hurst during England's finest hour, and by now we could have been talking about Sir David! I was particularly delighted, too, for John Aston, an intelligent, sound, undemonstrative boy who had known rough times at the hands of the fans. What an occasion for him to produce the display of a lifetime, and though he didn't show it particularly, John must have been ecstatic. At the opposite end of the spectrum, there was poor Denis Law, who was stuck in a hospital bed and was missed sorely, both on the pitch and at the bash afterwards. He would have rejoiced for the club, of course, but been utterly demoralised on a personal level. As to who would have missed out if Denis had been fit, only Matt would have known the answer to that. Some speculate that it would have been David Sadler, but that's unlikely because he played in all but one League game that term and his adaptability was invaluable. Others say it might have been Nobby, who was far from fully fit, but the very notion of his absence would have been incomprehensible. He was so important to me at that stage of my career, that I don't think I could have done without him. An academic question maybe, but enduringly fascinating for all that.

To return to London on 29 May 1968, as the collective euphoria washed over us, there was one aspect of our victory which filled me with dread, that of taking the trophy back to Manchester on an open-topped bus, surrounded by thousands of people. We had made a similar journey, albeit without any silverware, after the 1958 FA Cup Final and, no doubt for some impenetrable psychological reason, since then buses and crowds in conjunction have always been associated in my mind with the Munich crash.

There was no way I could have faced such an expedition, it would have destroyed me and brought back so much pain, so before the game I had laid my plans to avoid it. I had arranged for Teresa to take the car with our sons, Stephen and Geoffrey, to the home of the Cantwells in Peterborough, then drive on to Wembley and park somewhere near the stadium. Thus, after the reception, I was able to escape, and there were a couple of United youngsters – I'm sorry to say I can't remember their names – who were very grateful that I did. After attending the do, they had nowhere to sleep but we were able to give them the bedroom reserved for us at the hotel. We pulled out at about 4am, picked up the family from Noel's house, then drove home to Manchester, after which I went straight to Standerway Golf Club, where I was due to play that day for the Cheshire county team. Some people might have thought I had spurned the official homecoming just for the golf, but really that was rubbish, I could play golf at any time. In truth I was scared to reveal my reasons, even to Matt, who was such a plausible persuader that I feared he might talk me out of my little scheme. After all, he had talked me into many things down the years! As it was, I was the only player who didn't go on the bus and nobody ever asked me where I was, which was a trifle strange. For many years afterwards it haunted me that I might have given the impression that I simply hadn't bothered, but there never seemed to be an appropriate time to raise it with the Boss. That's something I regret. It's only a small thing, but I would have liked him to know that I cared as deeply as anyone about the greatest day in Manchester United's history, and was proud to have played my part in it.

*Evidence that my love affair with silverware started when I was very young. This is the Nut Grove football team from the St Helens area, which appears to have enjoyed a tolerably successful season round about 1935. I'm the little chap on the right of the front row and my dad is the goalkeeper.*

*Having thought my chance of a career with Manchester United might have slipped away, I decided to combine coalmining with playing part-time football for St Helens Town. The standard was pretty high and the Saints were a grand bunch of lads. Standing, left to right: Bold Thomas (trainer), Sonny Doyle, a young Bill Foulkes, Harry Critchley, Frank Booth, Frank Dillon, Alf Pennington, Bill Twist, Henniker (reserve). Sitting: Terry Garner, Sonny Byrne, George Friar (manager), Harry McCann, Albert Leadbetter.*

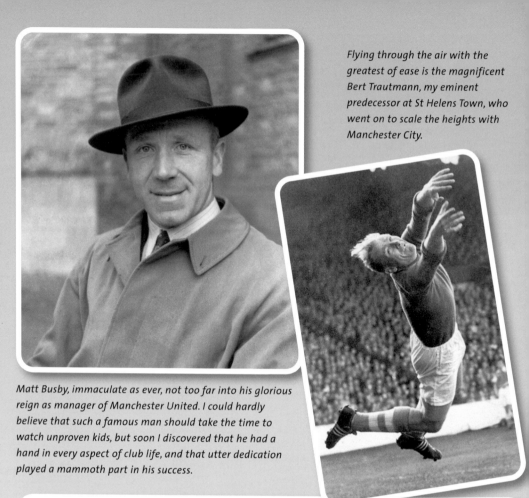

*Flying through the air with the greatest of ease is the magnificent Bert Trautmann, my eminent predecessor at St Helens Town, who went on to scale the heights with Manchester City.*

*Matt Busby, immaculate as ever, not too far into his glorious reign as manager of Manchester United. I could hardly believe that such a famous man should take the time to watch unproven kids, but soon I discovered that he had a hand in every aspect of club life, and that utter dedication played a mammoth part in his success.*

*Sharing the bench with team-mates of the highest quality during 1954/55. Left to right are Duncan Edwards (with a young friend), Dennis Viollet, the veteran Jack Rowley and myself.*

*A young man with the football world at his feet in the early 1950s.*

*Master and pupil. The slab of north-eastern granite that answered to the name of Allenby Chilton takes custody of the ball while I become tangled with the fallen Tottenham Hotspur marksman Len Duquemin at White Hart Lane in the mid 1950s.*

The Busby Babes in all their pomp, on their way to retaining the League title in 1956/57. Standing, left to right: Tommy Taylor, Mark Jones, Ray Wood, myself and Duncan Edwards. Sitting: Billy Whelan, Eddie Colman, Johnny Berry, Dennis Viollet, David Pegg and Geoff Bent, who was standing in for absent skipper Roger Byrne.

Having a laugh with little Eddie Colman, who will always hold a special place in my heart. I can understand the cricket bat, but I don't know where the sweeping brush came in!

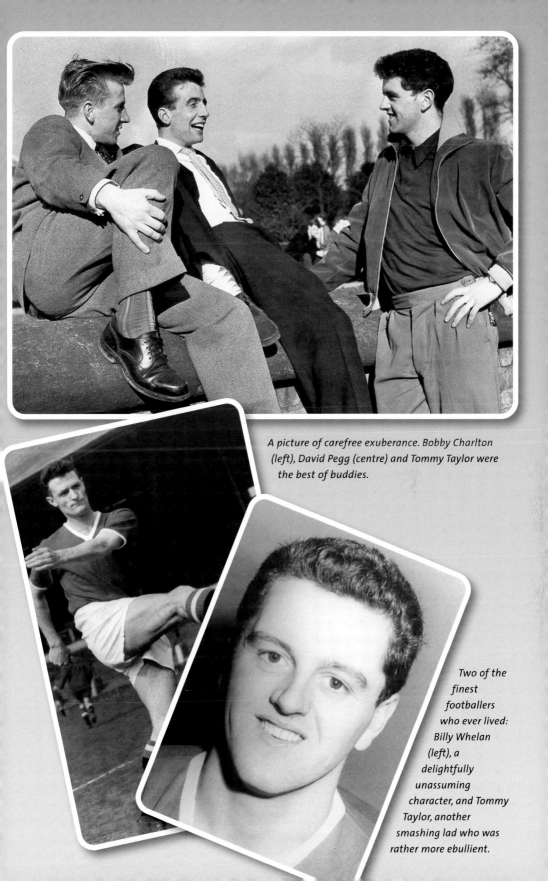

*A picture of carefree exuberance. Bobby Charlton (left), David Pegg (centre) and Tommy Taylor were the best of buddies.*

*Two of the finest footballers who ever lived: Billy Whelan (left), a delightfully unassuming character, and Tommy Taylor, another smashing lad who was rather more ebullient.*

*Practising my dead-ball technique back in 1958/59, when Old Trafford still had a skyline.*

*Kicking in at Old Trafford, in a study which might be familiar to collectors of bubble-gum cards in the late 1950s.*

Talking tactics, but not too seriously, before winning my one and only England cap against Northern Ireland at Windsor Park, Belfast, in October 1954. Left to right are manager Walter Winterbottom, a part-time mineworker named Bill Foulkes, skipper Billy Wright, Nat Lofthouse, Don Revie, Ray Wood, Johnny Haynes, Roger Byrne, John Wheeler, Ray Barlow and Bill Slater.

Matt Busby and Roger Byrne keep their clothes on while the rest of us quaff bubbly in the tub after clinching the 1956/57 League crown. Left to right are Johnny Berry, myself, Billy Whelan, Eddie Colman, David Pegg, Tommy Taylor and Bobby Charlton.

*What some might describe as my habitually stern expression belies the excitement we all felt at becoming the first English club to enter European competition.*

*The White Arrow, Alfredo di Stefano, soars skywards to aim a shaft at the Red Devils' heart in front of a full house during Real Madrid's European Cup semi-final first leg victory at the cavernous Bernabeu stadium in April 1957. United goalkeeper Ray Wood and skipper Roger Byrne are on the back foot, while Real winger Raymond Kopa loiters with intent.*

*In search of a ground-breaking League and FA Cup double, Matt Busby leads out Manchester United to face Aston Villa at Wembley in 1957. In line behind their manager are captain Roger Byrne, Johnny Berry, Jackie Blanchflower, Ray Wood (who was doomed to play a pivotal role in the distressing drama which was about to unfold), myself, Bobby Charlton, Tommy Taylor, Billy Whelan, Duncan Edwards and David Pegg. Tiny Eddie Colman is there, too, hidden behind big Duncan.*

*A typically tense moment in the nine-goal thriller at Highbury which marked the Busby Babes' valedictory appearance on English soil. United 'keeper Harry Gregg deals with a threat from Arsenal's Jimmy Bloomfield while Duncan Edwards stands guard. I'm arriving late on the scene, along with Mark Jones.*

*One of those pre-Munich days when flying was still pure pleasure to me. I'm on the threshold of the plane alongside Jackie Blanchflower with, in descending order, Duncan Edwards, Ray Wood and Mark Jones below us on the steps. Still with their feet on the ground are, left to right, trainer Tom Curry, Dennis Viollet (crouching), Billy Whelan, Eddie Colman, David Pegg, Tommy Taylor, Roger Byrne, Johnny Berry (behind Roger), reserve defender Peter Jones, Alex Dawson (mostly obscured), director WH Petherbridge and Matt Busby.*

# Manchester Evening News

27,654    TV & RADIO—PAGE 2    THURSDAY, FEBRUARY 6, 1958    PRICE 3d.

LATE
FINAL

# UNITED CUP XI
# CRASH: "28 DIE"

## Plunged into houses at Munich, exploded
## URVIVORS SAVED in
## LAZING WRECKAGE

of the greatest disasters to befall British football struck Manchester United this afternoon when the plane carrying the £350,000 wonder team crashed nich. At least 28 of the 40 aboard were killed; some reports said higher casualties were feared.

The plane, a B.E.A. Elizabethan, had just taken off and climbed to 60ft. when it crashed on the outskirts of the city.

The team was returning from Belgrade, where yesterday United drew 3-3 with Red Star, the Yugoslav champions, and so qualified for the semi-final of the European Cup.

The plane came down in the suburb of Kirchtrudering, exploding as it hit the ground.

The "Elizabethan" airliner.

United players and other members of the party board-ing the blazing airliner...

**WAS V.I.P. BABY ON THE PLANE?**

### BRIGHTON CONSPIRACY TRIAL
## Bennett shouts: I didn't swindle tax

PEOPL
KILLED
HOMES

ON BOARD

---

How news of the catastrophe at Munich was relayed back to Manchester. The final death toll was five fewer than at first feared.

A powerful image which captures the sickening depression which swept over me beside the broken body of our Elizabethan airliner in the mud and slush of Munich airport on the day after the crash.

Even back amid the wreckage, it seemed impossible to come to terms with the scale of the tragedy.

Leaving Munich at the start of the traumatic journey back to Manchester. Putting on a brave face between Harry Gregg and myself is the marvellous Jimmy Murphy, and we are accompanied by the kind travel courier who looked after us in the wake of the accident.

*A montage of images from Wembley 1958. Walking out for the game, with Stan Crowther behind me; introducing Freddie Goodwin to the Duke of Edinburgh; shaking hands with Bolton skipper Nat Lofthouse; beating Nat to the ball while Ronnie Cope covers; Nat celebrating with Bolton boss Bill Ridding while I contemplate our defeat;*

*The mood remains sombre as Manchester United and AC Milan emerge from the Old Trafford tunnel for the first leg of their European Cup semi-final in May 1958. That's me on the left followed by young Kenny Morgans, and Nils Liedholm is the Milan skipper.*

*The massed terraces of Hillsborough provide a dramatic backdrop as Tottenham's Jimmy Greaves shoots for goal despite my desperate lunge during our FA Cup semi-final meeting in 1962.*

The tension is palpable as Manchester United prepare to take their first flight as a team since the Munich air crash. Heading for an Amsterdam friendly in April 1959, in roughly descending order, are Matt Busby, Bobby Charlton, Harry Gregg, Wilf McGuinness, Freddie Goodwin, myself, Ronnie Cope, Albert Scanlon, Warren Bradley (partly obscured), assistant trainer Bill Inglis, Alex Dawson, Joe Carolan, trainer Jack Crompton and Albert Quixall.

I always relished aerial combat and here I am coming off best in a heading duel with Wolves' Peter Broadbent at Molineux, while Wilf McGuinness admires the view.

The side which performed a minor miracle in finishing as First Division runners-up in 1958/59, the first full campaign after Munich. Standing, left to right, are: Freddie Goodwin, myself, Harry Gregg, Ian Greaves and Joe Carolan. Sitting: Warren Bradley, Albert Quixall, Dennis Viollet, Bobby Charlton, Albert Scanlon and Wilf McGuinness.

Real Madrid made the grand gesture of playing United in a series of friendlies to keep us in the European swim while we rebuilt after Munich. Exchanging pennants with their skipper, Zarraga, in the Bernabeu was a memorable moment for me.

*Renewing my acquaintance with
Prince Philip, flanked by David Herd on my right, Denis Law and Paddy
Crerand on my left.*

*Lining up with the trophy are (back row) secretary Les Olive and directors Bill Young, Alan Gibson and Louis
Edwards, (middle row) Jimmy Murphy, trainer Jack Crompton, Shay Brennan, Harry Gregg, Maurice Setters,
David Gaskell, myself, David Herd and Matt Busby, (front row) Tony Dunne, Johnny Giles, Albert Quixall, Noel
Cantwell, chairman Harold Hardman, Denis Law, Bobby Charlton, Paddy Crerand and Nobby Stiles.*

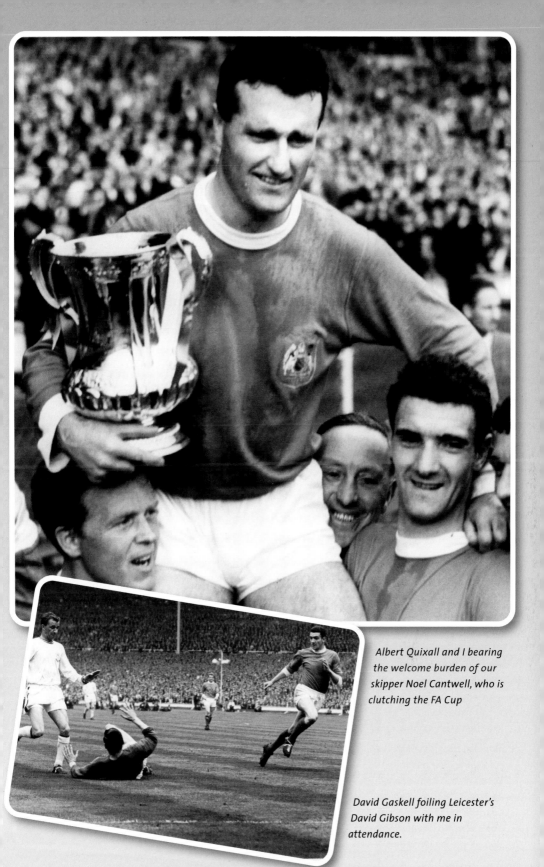

*Albert Quixall and I bearing the welcome burden of our skipper Noel Cantwell, who is clutching the FA Cup*

*David Gaskell foiling Leicester's David Gibson with me in attendance.*

*Goalkeeper Alex Stepney and myself stand by to repel the leaping Mike Doyle, one of the most passionately committed of all Manchester City men, at Maine Road in September 1967. We won 2-1 thanks to a Bobby Charlton brace, but City turned the tables at Old Trafford and had the last laugh by pipping us to the title.*

*The most important goal of my life. That's me in the middle of the top picture, astonishing all and sundry by slotting George Best's cross neatly into the Real Madrid net at the Bernabeu to secure our place in the 1968 European Cup Final. Brian Kidd might have expected a rebound, but all he has to do is jump for joy.*

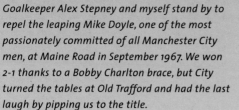

Goalkeeper Alex Stepney and myself stand by to repel the leaping Mike Doyle, one of the most passionately committed of all Manchester City men, at Maine Road in September 1967. We won 2-1 thanks to a Bobby Charlton brace, but City turned the tables at Old Trafford and had the last laugh by pipping us to the title.

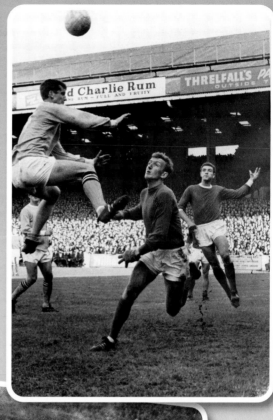

The most important goal of my life. That's me in the middle of the top picture, astonishing all and sundry by slotting George Best's cross neatly into the Real Madrid net at the Bernabeu to secure our place in the 1968 European Cup Final. Brian Kidd might have expected a rebound, but all he has to do is jump for joy.

*Champions again in 1964/65. Standing, left to right: Jack Crompton, myself, David Sadler, Pat Dunne, Shay Brennan, Graham Moore, Paddy Crerand, Noel Cantwell and Matt Busby. Sitting: John Connelly, Nobby Stiles, Bobby Charlton, Denis Law, Tony Dunne, David Herd and a promising young fellow name of George Best.*

*Believe it or not, the tumbling, white-shirted figure who has just nodded the ball into the Benfica net is me! It happened at Old Trafford in February 1966 and gave us a 3-1 lead in the first leg of a European Cup quarter-final, but yet more momentous events awaited in the return at the Stadium of Light.*

*Brandishing aloft the League Championship trophy as we embark on a triumphant lap of Old Trafford on the final Saturday of 1966/67. The revellers are, left to right, Bobby Charlton, Shay Brennan, John Aston, myself with George Best peering over my shoulder, Alex Stepney, Matt Busby, Paddy Crerand, Denis Law and Tony Dunne.*

I was never one to hold back when the ball was there to be won. Everton's Dennis Stevens, a cousin of Duncan Edwards, takes the brunt of a full-blooded Foulkes challenge during our Charity Shield encounter at Goodison Park in August 1963. We were crushed 4-0 by the League champions, after which Matt Busby made a few radical changes.

Surveying the fruits of my footballing labours, garnered during a long and incident-packed career with the greatest club in the world.

Mopping up with goalkeeper Pat Dunne after a Blackburn Rovers raid at Ewood Park in April 1965. That day Bobby Charlton plundered a hat-trick as we won 5-0, a crucial staging post on the way to the title.

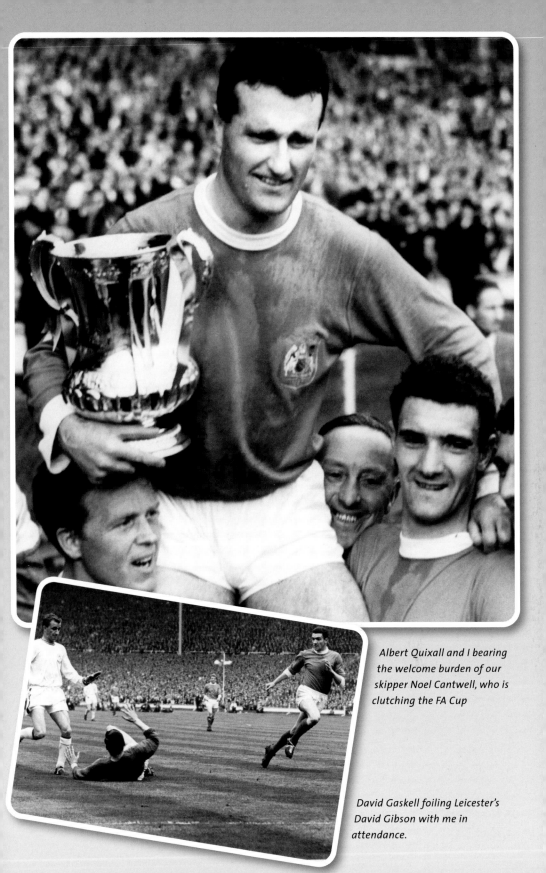

*Albert Quixall and I bearing the welcome burden of our skipper Noel Cantwell, who is clutching the FA Cup*

*David Gaskell foiling Leicester's David Gibson with me in attendance.*

*The gladiators acknowledge the crowd before battle commences in the European Cup Final at Wembley. John Aston (left) turned out to be the star of the show, George Best scored our vital second goal and I was detailed to look after Senor Torres.*

*Marching off alongside Bobby Charlton at the end of an emotional journey together*

*A special moment with The Boss.*

*Lifting the prize for which we had yearned for so long, with George Best on my right, Brian Kidd, Alex Stepney, David Sadler and Paddy Crerand to my left.*

*Admiring the trophy with Johnny Berry, one of our European pioneers whose career had ended at Munich.*

The team photograph for which United fans had been waiting for what seemed like an eternity. Back row, left to right: myself, John Aston, Jimmy Rimmer, Alex Stepney, Alan Gowling, David Herd. Middle row: David Sadler, Freddie Owen (assistant to the club secretary), Tony Dunne, Shay Brennan, Paddy Crerand, George Best, Francis Burns, chief scout Joe Armstrong, Jack Crompton. Front row: Jimmy Ryan, Nobby Stiles, Denis Law, Matt Busby, with the European Cup, Bobby Charlton, Brian Kidd, John Fitzpatrick.

The proudest of dads with Amanda, Stephen (the tall one at the back) and Geoffrey in 1968. For once the trophy was nothing to do with Manchester United, having been earned on the golf course. It's the St David's Gold Cup and I won it at Harlech that year.

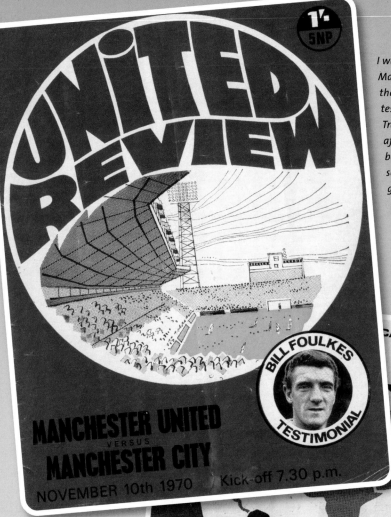

1'-
5NP

# UNITED REVIEW

BILL FOULKES
TESTIMONIAL

## MANCHESTER UNITED
VERSUS
## MANCHESTER CITY

NOVEMBER 10th 1970    Kick-off 7.30 p.m.

*I was honoured when Manchester City provided the opposition for my testimonial match at Old Trafford, some 15 months after I had kicked my last ball for the Red Devils in senior competition at the grand old age of 37.*

*A memento of one of the most unsavoury of sporting occasions. The World Club Championship should have been a showcase of all that's best in football; instead it was a disgrace.*

CAN CUP 1968

No. 9

MANCHESTER UNITED
OF ENGLAND
VERSUS
ESTUDIANTES
OF ARGENTINA
OCTOBER 16 1968

price 1/-

# UNITED REVIEW

THE OFFICIAL PROGRAMME OF MANCHESTER UNITED FOOTBALL CLUB

WINNERS OF THE EUROPEAN CHAMPIONS CUP COMPETITION 1968

Harry Gregg (left) and I both completed coaching stints at Old Trafford but not together. I spent four years on the United staff directly after retiring as a player, Harry returned later after experience elsewhere. Here we chew the fat with Tommy Cavanagh, who served as number-two to both Tommy Docherty and Dave Sexton.

Enjoying a rare moment of relaxation during my hectic first year in Chicago. The football was fulfilling, the family was happy and I might have stayed longer, but for lack of resources.

Tommy Docherty (centre), no doubt delivering a typically wicked one-liner to Tommy Cavanagh and myself when United visited Chicago in the mid 1970s.

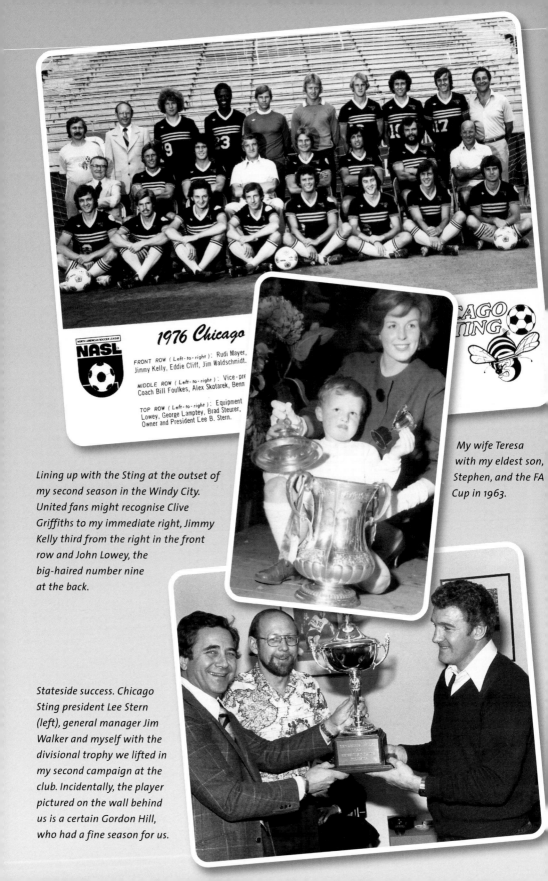

1976 Chicago

FRONT ROW ( Left-to-right ): Rudi Mayer,
Jimmy Kelly, Eddie Cliff, Jim Waldschmidt.

MIDDLE ROW ( Left-to-right ): Vice-pre
Coach Bill Foulkes, Alex Skotarek, Benn

TOP ROW ( Left-to-right ): Equipment
Lowey, George Lamptey, Brad Steurer,
Owner and President Lee B. Stern.

Lining up with the Sting at the outset of
my second season in the Windy City.
United fans might recognise Clive
Griffiths to my immediate right, Jimmy
Kelly third from the right in the front
row and John Lowey, the
big-haired number nine
at the back.

My wife Teresa
with my eldest son,
Stephen, and the FA
Cup in 1963.

Stateside success. Chicago
Sting president Lee Stern
(left), general manager Jim
Walker and myself with the
divisional trophy we lifted in
my second campaign at the
club. Incidentally, the player
pictured on the wall behind
us is a certain Gordon Hill,
who had a fine season for us.

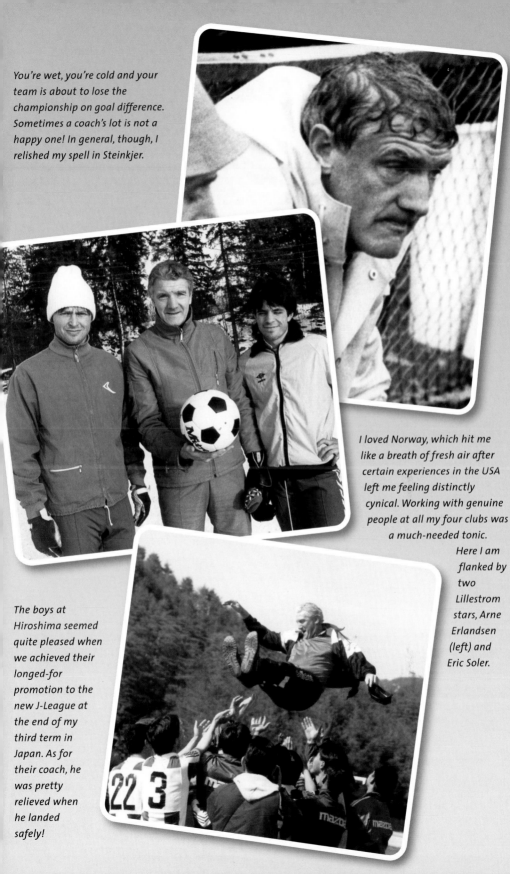

You're wet, you're cold and your team is about to lose the championship on goal difference. Sometimes a coach's lot is not a happy one! In general, though, I relished my spell in Steinkjer.

I loved Norway, which hit me like a breath of fresh air after certain experiences in the USA left me feeling distinctly cynical. Working with genuine people at all my four clubs was a much-needed tonic.

Here I am flanked by two Lillestrom stars, Arne Erlandsen (left) and Eric Soler.

The boys at Hiroshima seemed quite pleased when we achieved their longed-for promotion to the new J-League at the end of my third term in Japan. As for their coach, he was pretty relieved when he landed safely!

I get my hands on yet more silverware during a visit to Munich in 1997, though this particularly impressive bauble is not mine but the hard-earned property of my hosts, the world-famous Bayern.

*Making a United comeback (I wish) at Wembley in 1995, in a charity event prior to the FA Cup Final against Everton*

*A reunion with Sir Matt Busby and Bobby Charlton*

# Twelve

# **Winds of change**

**W**HEN MANCHESTER UNITED won the European Cup, I thought 'That's it! That caps my career. Now I'm satisfied.' And I'm afraid that too many people at Old Trafford took the same view. In my own case I think it was fair enough; I was in my 37th year and had won just about everything available to me over the previous one and a half decades. But that was no way for any club to think collectively and I am positive that it had a profoundly adverse effect on George Best, who at that point was the only rival to Pele as the finest footballer in the world. He was only 22, and should have had everything before him. Thus the prevailing air of 'job finished' can only have been supremely frustrating to him; it didn't tie in with his aspirations at all, and it must have contributed materially to his subsequent drinking problems. He was in a unique position, having become the game's first pop idol following his exploits at the Stadium of Light in 1966. By definition, then, there could be no appropriate role model, and with most of our players being a bit older, with families to look after, he was on his own to a great extent. In that climate, and along with a sense of professional letdown which must have been heightened by a lack of prospects at international level – being born in Belfast did him no favours at all career-wise – it is possible to see how he went off the rails. I know that in the end he lost control, that in a sense he threw it all away, but I have enormous sympathy for him, given his unique situation.

Let's be honest. United's team was in decline, even before defeating Benfica. Apart from George, none of the top men – Bobby, Denis, Paddy, Nobby – were going to get any better. Certainly I was ready for retirement, and Matt should have been ruthless enough to get rid of me, and probably one or two others, after Wembley '68. It was not that the older players didn't work or try, because people like that will give everything in every game, merely that the achievement of our long-sought holy grail brought about a loss of impetus. Certainly the same was true of the Boss, who was knighted in the wake of Wembley '68, and who could blame him after all he had survived and attained? Sadly, too, the quality of the youngsters he began to introduce was just not high enough to maintain our standards.

Still, 1968/69 was hardly an unmitigated disaster. Although we could finish no higher than 11th in the First Division, we took part in the World Club Championship and reached a second successive European Cup semi-final. I'm afraid the first-mentioned, the two-legged clash with Estudiantes de la Plata, was little more than a farce. Before the first meeting Nobby Stiles had been damned by his reputation, even the match programme described him as brutal, and he was duly victimised, being sent off ludicrously by the referee. Meanwhile the Argentinians kicked anything that moved while the official did nothing to protect us, and it was a wonder that we lost by only a single goal. As The Times writer Geoffrey Green put it beautifully, the Estudiantes players were 'hustlers, highly intelligent, markedly skilful men ... who could look after themselves in the darkest corners.' The return wasn't quite as bad, though George Best was dismissed along with Juan Medina after the Irishman had retaliated to a vicious foul, and we were always struggling after they scored an early goal through Juan Manuel Veron, the father of Juan Sebastian, whom United signed in 2001. We mustered a late reply from Willie Morgan, the gifted Scottish international winger acquired several months earlier from Burnley, but could do nothing further about the 2-1 aggregate deficit. The whole affair was a travesty of sport.

Back in Europe, we breezed past Waterford of the Republic of Ireland (10-2 over two games), survived a scare against Anderlecht (4-3) and dispatched Rapid Vienna comfortably (3-0) before running into AC Milan in the last four. Hopes of retaining the trophy had soared but, in a tumultuous atmosphere at the San Siro, we were forced to defend for most of the match, losing two goals – one of which should have been ruled out for handball – and John Fitzpatrick, who was sent off near the end. We lifted ourselves to give a spirited display back in Manchester, and when Bobby Charlton scored a wonderful goal after 70 minutes we had the Italians on the ropes. Soon afterwards we seemed to have equalised when Denis Law forced the ball over the line in a goalmouth scramble but the referee ruled that it had not gone in – and we were out. It was a bitter pill to swallow in a season of serial letdowns, albeit one in which I was content to be slipping out of the first-team reckoning as a player, while turning my attention to coaching the youngsters.

True, I didn't miss many European nights, but there were only ten League starts and I made no contribution to our run to the last eight of the FA Cup, having been replaced by promising rookie Steve James. In my mind, then, I had practically retired, but I was in for a rude shock on the morning of our quarter-final. I was in the middle of a television interview with Jimmy Hill at Maine Road when a taxi arrived to whisk me back to Old Trafford, where we were due shortly to face Everton. It turned out that Steve, a nice lad and a good centre-half, though rather lacking in self-belief, had frozen. He couldn't face the prospect of playing, and Matt told me that it looked as if I'd have to take his place. I didn't fancy that at all because I was nowhere near fit enough, so I thought I'd take the young man to one side and try a little psychology. I told him that he was a damned good player with all the equipment to do the job, that this was a marvellous opportunity and that if he didn't take it he might never get another. He was reluctant but eventually I talked him round and he did well in the game, even though United lost 1-0. Sadly, later on, Steve drifted out of contention having never made the most of his natural attributes. He must have been nursing some deep-seated uncertainty, a concept which was incomprehensible to me. It would never have entered my head not to play; I was a natural competitor while he was seeking excuses for not playing. However, this incident made me ponder the value of psychology in sport, and in later years it came into vogue. Too late, unfortunately, to save the career of Steve James.

While 1968/69 had proved anti-climactic, it did contain two momentous announcements. The first, in January, was that Sir Matt would be standing down as team manager in the summer, moving upstairs to become general manager; the second, three months later, was that 31-year-old Wilf McGuinness was promoted to take charge of selection, coaching, training and tactics. While having some idea of the burden he had carried, still I couldn't believe Matt's decision and I told him I thought he had made a mistake. He told me: 'You don't know, son' and shook his head. He was under pressure from somewhere, perhaps from family, and he didn't look happy about it. It was a time of transition, with an overhaul of the playing staff needed, and I believe he was better qualified to carry that out, perhaps over a couple of years, than anyone else. Maybe, after everything, he simply couldn't face the prospect of building his fourth team, and I can respect that. Certainly I don't blame him for wanting, perhaps needing, to step aside, but I am convinced that things would have been much better for Manchester United if he could have maintained full control. For a start it would have sent a positive signal to George Best that the club's ambitions matched his own; then he might have retained his enthusiasm and determination and, perhaps, would not have gone downhill.

What about Wilf? Well, his overall record did not prove to be the worst in the world, with three semi-finals – one in the FA Cup and two in the League Cup – in the space of one and a half seasons, and an eighth-place League finish. But, as Matt admitted later, he represented a colossal error of judgement. I had known Wilf since his days as a United schoolboy and there was no doubt that he was a Red Devil through and through. He would have bled for the club,

probably would have died for it. As a player he had been Duncan
Edwards' stand-in, and there had been no limit to his enthusiasm and
aggression, courage and devotion. Unfortunately the same cannot be
said of his finesse or of his luck. He had won a couple of England
caps and was building a reputation as a doughty wing-half when his
leg, and his career, was smashed in one mistimed tackle. After that he
became a coach at Old Trafford, later helping Alf Ramsey in the
England set-up, but there was no way he was experienced enough to
succeed Sir Matt Busby. He was younger than some of the senior
players, he lacked authority over them, and there were one or two
who might have resented him for that. Whatever the truth of the
situation, I felt he never earned their respect and he made some
extremely suspect decisions, for instance the dropping of Law and
Charlton for the same match. Wilf was never short of words but he
didn't use them judiciously. Sometimes he just went on and on, and
things got out of control. Where club politics were concerned, and
there was no shortage of them at Old Trafford, he never had a prayer.
Conceivably he might have stood a chance had he gone somewhere
else and proved himself first, but I'm far from convinced.

Matt and Jimmy Murphy asked me to chat with Wilf about the
possibility of me working alongside him, perhaps in the way that the
pair of them had combined so successfully in the past, but the new
boss made it plain that he wasn't interested in using me at that level.
I wasn't too dismayed because my own view was that I wasn't ready
for management at that stage.

Wilf's only full season at the helm coincided with my last as a
player, although really I should have stopped much earlier because
my knee was in such an appalling state. The only reason I didn't was
that United kept asking me to bale them out when younger
replacements did not come up to scratch. As it was I played the first
three games of the campaign, my farewell being an unhappy one at
home to Southampton on 16 August 1969, when we lost 4-1 and the
Saints' centre-forward, Ron Davies, scored all the goals. It was an
infuriating manner in which to depart after nearly 700 games, all at

the top level, because I was in no condition to give a fair account of myself. Davies was a fine player but he had never bothered me unduly in the past. Now I was doing my club a favour and being punished for it. At least, though, there could be no further argument that, with my 38th birthday approaching, I would have to concentrate exclusively on coaching the reserves.

In June 1970, Wilf shed the title of chief coach to be made team manager, but a sustained sequence of poor results and a poisonous atmosphere behind the scenes led to an inevitable conclusion that December – he was sacked. He was shocked by the decision, his health suffered as a result and I felt immensely sorry for him, but he had to go. A lot of critics blamed Matt, reckoning that he made Wilf's task impossible merely by his presence at the club, but I disagree. I was there all the time and I observed no interference. I will admit to a certain surprise when Matt temporarily resumed the reins, but the subsequent upturn in results was entirely predictable. Quite simply the players gave him their respect, they were ready to bust a gut for him. They never did that as a unit with Wilf; I'd say that the younger fellows gave him their all, because he presented many of them with their first-team opportunities, but he was a long, long way from rejoicing in the universal support of his entire staff.

Part of my remit during that troubled period was helping to keep George Best on the straight and narrow. More and more frequently, he was yielding to the temptation of off-the-field distractions, of which booze was certainly the most destructive. But also he was involved with several clothes boutiques, a racehorse, a TV documentary on his life, fast cars, and a seemingly never-ending procession of beautiful girls. By his own subsequent admission, there were periods when he partied around the clock, and the club became increasingly worried. The anxiety came to a head when George let himself down in an incident with referee Jack Taylor at the end of United's 2-1 defeat by Manchester City at Maine Road in the first leg of the League Cup semi-final in December 1969. Frustrated by the defeat, and incensed by the award of a late decisive penalty, it seems

George lost his rag and knocked the ball out of the official's hands. As a result he was banned from playing for four weeks, and the management was fearful that he might let himself go physically during the ensuing lay-off. Thus he was told to train with the reserves, under my watchful eye. Now I would never have presumed to talk to George about football, but I knew something about fitness and could see that although he was a tremendous natural athlete, he was in need of a concentrated tune-up. I had a friend called Tommy Hamilton who ran a gym in Stretford and I used to go there often, sometimes doing weight training against Matt's wishes. It wasn't that I was rebelling, just that I felt I knew my body better than anyone else. This was before the days of multi-gyms and the place looked like a torture chamber with gear that Tommy had put together himself. He was way ahead of his time, and could have made a fortune if he'd put a patent on it. George's face was a picture when he walked in, but I explained that it wasn't a punishment, merely a means to get him into top condition.

My regime consisted of a morning's training at The Cliff, followed by weights at Tommy's in the afternoon, finishing off with a jog – and George did it! I'm not saying he enjoyed it, exactly, but he amazed me with his natural strength and power, and after four weeks he was in the best shape he'd been in his life. And, being George, he announced his return in the most dramatic and flamboyant manner imaginable, by shooting six goals past Northampton Town in an FA Cup tie. It was an astonishing feat by an incredible footballer, and my mind boggles at what he might have achieved had he not succumbed to temptation. We had plenty of chance to chat during that month of hard graft, and I advised him constantly to step out of the limelight, to make life easier for himself. I told him that if he wanted to go into town, then to do it discreetly, leave the huge white Jaguar at home. He would nod and say 'okay', then head off to Slack Alice or wherever he was going and park his flashy motor at the front door, so the whole wide world knew where he was and what he was doing. That was George and there was no changing him. God knows, Matt

Busby tried hard enough, so I suppose there was little chance that I would succeed.

After Wilf had gone, I continued in control of the reserves under Matt and as the club searched for a new manager for the start of 1971/72, I examined my own ambitions. Friends had told me that I might be the man for the job, but still I was not ready for it. I loved the game and wanted to be out there on the field, helping the players, rather than move behind a desk. If the timing had been different, then who knows? As it was, I thought perhaps the top two candidates would be Jock Stein of Celtic and Don Revie of Leeds, men who had known success with big clubs and who would not be overawed by United. However, the job went to Frank O'Farrell, who had proved himself to be a steady boss with Leicester City and he arrived with an admirable ready-made assistant in Malcolm Musgrove. I thought there would still be a role for me with the reserves but I was given an early shock when Frank sent for me and told me to look for another job. He had a fine reputation as a coach and I had been looking forward to learning from him, but now it seemed that my hopes were in ruins. Still, I wasn't going to let it go at that, so I told him a few home truths about the club. Suddenly, to my astonishment, he told me to disregard what he had said and that he wanted me to stay. I left that office a very confused man: one minute I'd been sacked and the next I was in a job again. Later I told Matt what had happened and he just shook his head. After that I had no idea what to expect of Frank, but he emerged as a quiet, authoritative fellow, a decent guy but very withdrawn, and I don't think he ever became close to the players. For all that, he started brilliantly and United surged to the top of the table in the autumn, but George was carrying the team more than ever before, and a one-man show can never work for long. Inevitably, they blew up so comprehensively that they could hardly win a match. George took it badly, and I believe it was around this time that his drinking began to get out of hand. Whatever, the rapidly deteriorating Best situation became a festering sore for poor O'Farrell, who found club politics difficult to handle and, after making a disastrous start to 1972/73, he was dismissed and replaced by Tommy Docherty. It was an unhappy time, with a lot of acrimony between Frank and Matt, and the atmosphere around the place was terrible.

At this point I had gained coaching qualifications and thought I might be offered the post of assistant manager, but as invariably happens, the new man brought his own number-two, in this case Tommy Cavanagh. Now the Doc upset a lot of people at Old Trafford; no one would claim that he was whiter-than-white in every respect, and certainly he made mistakes. But equally no one can reasonably deny that he did a marvellous job of transforming a very poor United team which had begun to slide towards the end of my playing days and had been getting worse ever since. Admittedly, after averting relegation in '73, he took them down the following season, which seemed catastrophic at the time, but to be brutally honest, it was just what they needed. The club was in a terrible mess, with a lot of players who weren't good enough to be there, and he produced an exhilarating new side which hit English football like a breath of fresh air, bouncing back to the First Division at the first attempt. Certainly I enjoyed the entertaining football espoused by the Doc and Cav, and I relished working under them. Ultimately Docherty was dismissed in farcical fashion, apparently over his love affair with Mary Brown, the wife of club physio Laurie. Without going into the rights and wrongs of that, such things happen every day and it had no bearing on his work. If that was all there was to it, then he should have stayed, but I believe it was a mere excuse and that it was a political sacking. I am convinced that certain powerful people within the club wanted him out, for what precise reasons I know not.

By then, though, I had long gone, unable to remain at Manchester United, where I had spent almost a quarter of a century. The reason why? They wouldn't pay me a decent wage!

# Thirteen

# Into the wide blue yonder

**M**ONEY, OR the conspicuous lack of it, forced me into a previously unthinkable course of action – the leaving of Old Trafford. For a couple of years I had coached on a player's contract, which was around £70 a week and acceptable enough in those days. But then I was shifted to a formal coach's agreement, which was only £38, at a time when the cost of living was rocketing. I took my problem to Matt Busby, by then a club director and still a hugely powerful figure, and told him the money was hopelessly inadequate. I explained that, as a family man with three children, I just couldn't get by on that. It was starvation wages. But Matt always had a blind spot where cash was concerned, shades of his upbringing again, and nothing was done. By then it was 1974 and I had been with Manchester United for 20 years as a player, plus four more running the reserves. Recently I had been on FA coach courses, so I'd found out what other clubs were paying, but that cut no ice. The Boss – as I always thought of him – even had the cheek to advise me not to leave until I'd got another job, yet offered no help in getting me fixed up elsewhere. Instead I was indebted to Bob Paisley, who had just replaced Bill Shankly as manager of our greatest rivals, Liverpool, for pointing me in the right direction. Bob had heard they were seeking coaches in the United States, where football appeared to be about to take off in a big way with the launch of the new North American Soccer League, and he put me in touch with the right man.

Obviously it was a colossal wrench to walk away from Old Trafford, but I had to face the fact that it wasn't the same club I had grown up in. There had been so many staff changes, a lot of people were ahead of me in the pecking order, and the old atmosphere seemed to have vanished.

One incident in the early 1970s, though insignificant in itself, was indicative of how the feel of the place had changed. It was in the run-up to Christmas and there was a do for the coaching staff in the city centre. I was there with Teresa and at one point she said: 'Isn't that Brian Kidd over there?' Now I couldn't see because the figure disappeared around a corner, but I knew Brian shouldn't be present as the team had a match the next day. However, I thought no more about it, just got on with enjoying the evening. But the next morning as I went in to training I saw someone lurking under the stand, and I was amazed when Matt Busby emerged abruptly from the shadows. Without the slightest preamble he snapped: 'What's all this about Kidd being out last night?' I told him that I knew the policy but that I hadn't seen Brian, which was the truth. He made it clear that he didn't believe me, as he replied: 'It's your job to tell me if players don't do what they're told. Don't ever do that again.' It was the way he said it, his menacing tone, which perturbed me. After practically worshipping the man for more than 20 years, I was upset to think that he felt I was being disloyal to him. I guess he felt under pressure, but it struck me forcibly then that no one could be Mr Nice Guy and keep their thumb on an empire like his, and it reinforced my growing notion that it was time for me to change direction. So it was against that sort of background that the news of my American opportunity reached me in the form of a phone call from Teresa while I was at Newcastle with United's reserves. I had reached such a low ebb that I exclaimed: 'Thank God.' I was so delighted and relieved at the prospect of starting a new chapter in my life that I was ready to travel 3,000 miles with a smile on my face.

It was the autumn of 1974 and, having agreed a deal to coach Chicago Sting, a new club with no players, immediately I found myself extremely busy, having only a few months in which to put together a whole team. In addition I scouted unfamiliar Second Division opponents for Tommy Docherty as he set about leading United back to the top flight at the first attempt, and I enjoyed a temporary stint as manager of Witney Town. My time in the Southern League was fruitful, as I learned a little bit about being in charge of a club and we went 17 games without defeat. They were lovely people and I enjoyed my time there. Of course, my wider scouting activities were doubled-edged; Manchester United benefited, but also I turned up quite a few players for Sting, my most outstanding find being Millwall's Gordon Hill, later to become an Old Trafford hero. My squad also contained a couple of United youngsters, midfielder Jimmy Kelly and striker John Lowey, and half a dozen from Tranmere Rovers, including Ronnie Moore.

I arrived in Chicago just before Christmas – boy, was it cold? – and was met by the owner and chairman, Lee Stern, a hard-nosed businessman who plunged me straight into a high-powered press conference in which I was expected to outline Sting's plans, even though I was yet to recruit any personnel. In fact, it was a doddle, because none of the media-men knew anything about the game at that time. They just listened to what I had to say, most unlike the pressmen of my experience! Thereafter I embarked on a period of shuttling back and forth across the Atlantic, as well as scouring Europe and the USA itself as I assembled my squad. In the end I think I had a fair selection, which included some local footballers, and in our first season we finished second in our division. The following year we kicked off against the heavily-hyped New York Cosmos, whose line-up read like a who's who of international football, containing names such as Pele and Franz Beckenbauer. Undaunted, and boosted by the arrival of my ex-United team-mate Willie Morgan, we beat them 2-0.

That infuriated the publicity men, who needed the stars to do as well as possible to widen the appeal of the product, but I wasn't playing that particular game. We won the division that season, then came second again in the following campaign as my coaching philosophy of attacking football – the same pass-and-move ethos which I had learned so long ago with the Busby Babes – paid gratifying dividends. The family had settled well, too, enjoying the American way of life, and to this day they treasure memories from our time in the 'Windy City'. One which sticks with me is of a stroll around town to show them the sights on one of my rare afternoons off. We were on a massive six-lane highway and became fascinated by the adroit work of a traffic cop in the middle of the busiest crossroads I have ever seen. We had been watching him for a few moments when suddenly he held up his hands in all directions and brought the traffic to a standstill. As he marched towards us with loads of queueing motorists beginning to blast their horns, I turned to Teresa and said: 'It looks like we're in trouble, but what have we done?' He just gave me a big grin, clapped me on the shoulder and said: 'Coach, you've done a great job. Keep up the good work.' Then he ushered us safely across the road, completely ignoring the fury of the people he had kept waiting. Years later, when Ron Atkinson heard the story, he threw up his hands and said: 'I'd love that to happen to me.' I suppose it would have been right up his street but, although it seems a great moment as I look back, I admit to being a trifle embarrassed.

In the end there were unacceptable financial restrictions on the Chicago operation and in 1977 I took the chance of a fresh start in Tulsa, where a new team franchise was arriving from Hawaii. Thus the Tulsa Roughnecks were born, once again I recruited players from all over – including Colin Boulton, a wonderful goalkeeper who had done well for Derby County – and we began to thrive. However, all too soon, I became aware of what seemed to be distinctly shady dealings behind the scenes. I was going to have no truck with anything which smacked of corruption and so I got out as quickly as possible. It was a pity because the football was going well and I was enjoying other aspects of the life, including a TV slot as a soccer talkshow host, but I gave it up and returned to England in 1978.

I was offered various Third Division management jobs but I didn't
fancy them and spent 18 months out of work, gradually bringing
down my golf handicap, before Phil Woosnam – the former West
Ham, Aston Villa and Wales inside-forward who had become a top
administrator in the USA – came on the phone, suggesting that I call
a guy who had bought a club franchise in San Jose, California. It
turned out to be an enterprising Yugoslavian named Milan Mandaric,
later to become chairman of Portsmouth, who met me in Manchester
and we struck an agreement. As ever on the American scene, I was
asked to look for players and my first thought was that George Best,
who had long since departed from Old Trafford, was playing for
Hibernian. I saw him line up against Celtic and it wasn't the Best I
knew. He looked like a skeleton, horribly frail and unfit, and he
hardly got a kick of the ball. His private life was upside down at the
time, his drinking was becoming ever more serious and it appeared
that he barely knew what was happening. However, I felt that if we
transported him to a more favourable environment, then he could be
an asset for San Jose Earthquakes, and although Mandaric was
sceptical, he left it to me. Pretty soon George was training in a
magnificent climate. Suddenly, this was more like the player I knew.
There was a sparkle in his eyes, some colour in his face and before
long the old confidence flooded back. As the season went on, George
looked better and better. Another enormous bonus was the
recruitment of Colin Bell, whose outstanding career for Manchester
City and England had been curtailed by injury. I thought that even if
he was hobbling, Colin would be more effective than most of the
alternatives available to me in San Jose, and he agreed to give it a go.
As it turned out, his experience brought crucial stability to the side,
everything went through him, and the team started to gel. I could
hardly believe that I'd got Best and Bell together in the same side,
but it wasn't all smooth sailing. For one thing, it was not a great
financial situation, it was all rather hand-to-mouth. I used to pay
George on a Monday after the game – I wouldn't pay him beforehand
in case he got drunk and didn't turn up. And that was another major

problem: it was during his San Jose sojourn that George was diagnosed as an alcoholic. In the end, after a year in California, I left and he stayed. I had to go because of the money, quite simply I was getting nowhere near enough, though it was not easy to leave a side that was playing such lovely football. We were in mid-table, and drawing good crowds, many of the Latin locals knowing far more about the game than in other areas of the States. Beyond that, I felt a certain sadness in leaving North America because football had been very close to taking off in a big way. I'm convinced that it would have done if the NASL had secured a major TV contract which took the game into people's living rooms. But all the contracts which mattered rested with American football, basketball and baseball; we were up against ruthless men, big businessmen with a lot of power, and in the end I don't think our league handled it that well.

On bidding farewell to the States, at first I returned to England but then, in 1980, I embarked on the next leg of my coaching odyssey, this time fetching up in Norway, where I was to spend seven fascinating years, thanks to contacts provided by my old friend Nils Olaf Krinstad, a long-time Manchester United supporter. After re-crossing the Atlantic with a cynical attitude following a series of traumatic financial experiences, it was wonderful to make a fresh start among people with such a refreshing passion for the game. My first stop was in the little fishing community of Brynne, perched picturesquely by the North Sea. There I found innocence and enthusiasm, determination and integrity, just what I needed to get me going again. It's no word of a lie to say that I was enchanted.

I found the Norwegians to be a naturally hard-working people who keep themselves fit, and they were very receptive to my efforts. Brynne were a small Third Division club and the idea was that I would spend a season there, just to find out if I liked the scene, before moving on to bigger clubs. Yet there was one moment during that first term when the prospect of a return to my spiritual home, Old Trafford, loomed suddenly and tantalisingly on my horizon. One day I was chatting to the coach of Kristiansund, the former Charlton

Athletic and Bolton goalkeeper Charlie Wright, when he said: 'Would you believe what has happened to United? What a mess!' I had got a little out of touch with the English situation, so he explained that Dave Sexton had been sacked and, according to the soccer grapevine, various people had been linked with the job – Brian Clough, Lawrie McMenemy, Bobby Robson – but that none of them wanted it. After reflecting on Charlie's news, it grieved me to think of the club going downhill so fast and I had a notion to get involved. And I had a more specific idea, too! So I called Martin Edwards, with whom I have always had a decent rapport, and suggested that he asked Bobby Charlton to apply for the boss' role while I would come as coach. My job would be to prepare the team, Bobby would select and all the rest of it. Martin sounded interested and he got hold of Bobby, but when my old team-mate contacted me the following day, it put an end to the possibility. He told me that he was going in a completely different direction and did not want to re-enter football management (he'd had a short spell with Preston in the 1970s). In the event, Martin took on Ron Atkinson, who did pretty well by winning the FA Cup twice but falling down, in my opinion, in two crucial areas. He didn't exercise sufficient discipline and he didn't have a youth policy, areas in which Alex Ferguson would excel in later years. Would Martin have given Bobby and myself the job if Bobby had been of a different mind? Who knows, but it would have been interesting if he had.

As it was, after keeping Brynne in the Third Division on a shoestring, I switched to Steinkjer, a top Second Division club situated idyllically on a fjord feeding on to the North Sea, not far from the city of Trondheim. Here I found the same delightful attitude, but it was a bigger club with much more lavish facilities, which allowed for rather more ambition. Early on, though, I did have one embarrassing experience when, not accustomed to the extreme cold, I couldn't understand why the players were not training outdoors so I went for a run, almost to set an example. But that cold got to my lungs, made me ill for two weeks, and I heard one of my new charges mutter: 'I think we've got an old granny here!' I thought: 'We'll see about that' and pretty soon he was admitting that he'd got that wrong as I put them through a searching fitness programme. To be fair they did everything I asked and the team went from strength to strength. While using the same group of players, we moved from below halfway in the previous campaign to battling for the promotion and the crowds increased dramatically. In the end we missed out by a tiny percentage of goal average and that was because our rivals Brann Bergen won their final match 9-0. I just couldn't believe that margin in a highly competitive professional league, and I smelt a rat. I had no proof of corruption, but I was feeling bitter, which made me receptive to tempting offers from both Lillestrom and Rosenborg, two of Norway's leading clubs.

I opted for Lillestrom, believing that I could make a real name for myself with them, and in my first season we enjoyed considerable success. Playing some beautiful football, we finished second in the League, missing out narrowly on taking the title, and we played in the UEFA Cup, beating Locomotiv Leipzig at home before folding in Germany. As I expected, that proved an ideal platform for the subsequent campaign which we began brilliantly, going about eight points clear by halfway, and that was unknown in Norway. We were so superior to the rest, we were utterly confident and all our hard graft was paying off. I felt it was a privilege to work with such dedicated guys who all wanted success so much. But then our fortunes were transformed when the national squad took my six best players for the Olympic and I was left to fill the gaps with youngsters from the junior teams. The first-choice men returned when there were only a handful of games left, but they were shattered mentally and physically, and we finished fifth. The FA compensated the club financially but that was no consolation for me. I wanted to win the Championship and I was totally disillusioned by the whole affair.

Unfortunately money runs the game everywhere and, when I mulled over the experience, I realised that although Lillestrom was a lovely club, and was run on impeccably professional lines, it didn't really generate much cash. I thought I'd better find out where there was more finance, which would enable me to achieve more, and I accepted an offer from Viking Stavanger, a mighty club with a palatial stadium and terrific new training facilities. I moved in spite of warnings that the club was subject to serial infighting and power struggles, and to begin with things could not have progressed more smoothly. We made rapid progress in the table, from near the bottom to third place with a quarter of the campaign left to run. I wanted to sign three new players, putting it to the board that it would cost peanuts and that if we signed them we had a real chance of taking the title. They refused, I told them they were not living up to their pledges when I arrived, and I resigned. They paid me all that was owed, they even apologised for their conduct, but having had that showdown I was unable to get another job in Norway's top division. A little later I made a brief return to Steinkjer, but it was ill-advised, as it usually is when you return to the scene of former success. The first time it's something new, refreshing, different; it's rare to reproduce that kind of spark and, although I kept them in their division and they were satisfied with me, I wanted better than that, which is why I left.

My departure from Norway, though it left me a little sad in some respects, at least lifted the frequent pressure of long journeys home to England by sea and land (even though it was 30 years on from Munich I still avoided air travel wherever possible). One of those trips turned into a nine-hour nightmare as a heavy storm tossed the overnight boat from Oslo to Keel in Germany. I spent most of the time in my cabin, being lifted from my bed to the roof by the mountainous seas. Every time we went down I thought we were never going to come up. At Munich everything had been over in a flash but this seemed to go on forever and I had never been so scared in my life. Certainly, though, it brought back all the horror of the accident, and I still shudder to think of it.

Safely back in England in 1988, I took stock of my situation. At 56 I felt I was far from finished, but was adamant that if I was going to remain in the game, I wanted the football without the politics.

Some thrive on the rat race, could hardly exist without it, but I hated it and determined to avoid it in the future. Right on cue, along came an offer which sounded tailor-made for me. The Mazda club in Hiroshima, Japan, needed a coach, having recently been relegated to their Second Division. Their need was pressing because the new J-League was on the horizon, which would catapult Japanese football into the professional era, and to the Mazda company it was essential that they did not languish in the wake of fierce rivals such as Toyota. Having been guided towards the post by United supporter Mr Tsuneo Ito, who became a long-standing friend, that first season I worked with home-grown players and we did well. In fact, we topped the table at one point, only to be squeezed out of promotion by a Toyota-backed club which included overseas footballers of the calibre of Zico, the famous Brazilian.

For the second season I expected promotion, having signed some English players – including former Manchester United man Scott McGarvey from Oldham – but in the end we failed by a decimal point. With three games to go we were in a very strong position and the Mazda people began to get over-confident, even holding a celebratory dinner, which I told them was both premature and an unwanted distraction. It seemed to me that even the players thought they had won it, when nothing was certain, and duly it slipped agonisingly away. I was horrified; clearly I needed a heart-to-heart talk with the club officials if there was to be any future in our relationship but I knew I must remain level-headed. Accordingly I told them that I had enjoyed the experience, I was hugely impressed with their set-up, their support and their enthusiasm, but – and it was a big but – I had to be in total control of team affairs. I said that if they placed their complete trust in me, did exactly what I said, especially during the crucial run-in period, then I would both be happy to stay and confident that we could reach the J-League. Their leader, a polite little fellow but with eyes like steel, replied: 'Mr Bill, would you leave the room?' Ten minutes later I was recalled and he said: 'Mr Bill, yes Mr Bill, we have thought and we will do everything in our power to help you. Thank you for what you have done, and here is an extra bonus.' That was not necessary, but it was much appreciated, and the story had a happy ending. In my third term in Hiroshima, we achieved that coveted promotion in time to be part of the prestigious new tournament, and my employers spoke ecstatically of the future, which included changing the name of the club to San Frecce Hiroshima. They had a magnificent general manager named Mr Kazuo Imanishi, without whose support and advice we would never have achieved what we did. I wasn't surprised when he went on to become a leading official with the Japan under-21 side – those lads couldn't be in better hands.

There was to be no league in the season following our triumph, just cup competitions and wholesale team-building while finishing touches were put to the new set-up, but now I found myself at a major crossroads. Teresa and I loved the life in Japan. The country is imbued with a strong family ethos, in general it is scrupulously clean, and there appeared to be very little violence. It was safe to walk anywhere in Hiroshima, day or night. Admittedly Tokyo was crowded but Hiroshima wasn't, and the transport system was magnificently efficient. But increasingly we became aware that something was missing. I was approaching 60 and, to be blunt, we were both getting homesick. With three children and six grand-children, it didn't feel right to be on the other side of the world. You get to a stage in life when you wonder if you're going to see them again. The kids would come over to see us but it was a hell of a way to bring them. In the end we felt it was too far, and we made the momentous decision to make a permanent return to England. It was tough, because the Japanese had such big plans of which they wanted me to be a part. To be honest, I was a bit scared of telling them. In the end, though, they understood my position and I helped to fix them up with a successor, Stuart Baxter, a good coach and a splendid fellow. Happily, I retained a strong link with the Japanese club, acting as European scout, a role which I fulfilled into the new millennium. Later on I took parties of Japanese footballers, 15 to 16 year-olds, to

Manchester United, Manchester City, Bolton, Blackburn and Stockport, organising games with the English junior sides and sessions with the club coaches. Undoubtedly the standard of Japanese players is rising all the time, and I can foresee only a bright future for them, especially in the light of the 2002 World Cup.

Recently, too, though now in my 70s, I have worked for Football For Life, a coaching initiative for youngsters, in conjunction with the Manchester FA, spending up to five days a week at local colleges. It was way back in the 1950s that I became a Busby Babe, and it's an enormous pleasure to be putting something tangible back into the game more than half a century later.

# Fourteen

# A few reflections

CONTRARY TO what many people may surmise, the best thing that ever happened to me was not joining Manchester United. It was marrying Teresa. Without her I would never have enjoyed my gloriously long, successful career in football, and I say that without the slightest shadow of a doubt.

Teresa is a very strong character, and she has had to be. Playing football at the top level entails giving up a huge portion of your home life. Apart from the matches, there is so much travelling and training involved, and I have to admit that I didn't really see my three children grow up. I regretted it, sorely at times, but it was my job. I missed birthdays, school plays, sports days, the lot, but Teresa was always there for Stephen, Geoffrey and Amanda. She was magnificent, week after week and year after year.

Professional sport can exact an appalling price from those who devote their life to it. So many marriages crack under the constant pressure, but we worked hard at our relationship – as every couple has to – and we were fine.

In saying that, I realise that Teresa gave up a great deal to become Mrs Bill Foulkes. She has a fine brain, she is a resolute personality and she is an astute judge of character, so I am certain she could have been a successful businesswoman in her own right had she not elected the rocky path of footballer's wife.

I was so lucky to meet her when I did at a dance in Liverpool, her home city, back in 1950. I was already with United but she knew nothing about football and it quickly became apparent that she had little interest in sport, which suited me fine. Spending time with Teresa enabled me to forget my work totally, rather than allowing it to become an obsession, as so many footballers do.

Unfortunately she fell ill with tuberculosis soon after we got together and she was forced to spend 18 months in a body plaster, lying down all the time to prevent curvature of her spine. It was a traumatic period because her life was in danger and only the advent of a new drug saved her. Because I was working down the mine and training constantly during the week, then playing matches on Saturdays, only on Sundays could I visit her in hospital on the Wirral, but I never missed a trip.

We married in January 1955 but then, just as I believed I was to become a regular full-time professional, I was conscripted into the Army for National Service, which meant that I hardly saw her for two years. Teresa had recovered from TB by then and it was just as well because we were short of money and she had to go to work. She coped brilliantly, just as she did after the arrival of Stephen in December 1958, Geoffrey in January 1962 and Amanda in January 1963, working damned hard to bring up the three of them virtually on her own. Happily they inherited many of her characteristics and they have all done well in their chosen professions, Stephen excelling as an architect, Geoffrey as a television producer and musical event promoter, and Amanda in marketing, until she opted to spend time at home with her children and her horses. We are both very proud of them, as we are of our seven grandchildren: Jessica, Edward, Lewis, Matthew, Adam, Harvey and Philippa. Family was the reason we returned to England from Japan and my advice to anybody in football is unequivocal – give your all to the game but never lose sight of the fact that nothing is more important than your family.

I must admit, though, that another interest entered my life in the early 1960s, one that has almost verged on obsession at times. Having passed 30, I figured that my football-playing days must be limited and so I looked around for another sport. My first thought was for cricket so I had a chat with a good friend, Norman Brierley, a member of Hale Barns CC. He was quite persuasive so I bought all the gear, joined Norman's club and did reasonably well as batsman, bowler and wicketkeeper. It seemed I was a natural all-rounder. I had a good eye, I could hit the ball hard and far, and I recalled Mr Churchward, my schooldays sports mentor, once saying to me after a particularly long innings: 'Bill, you'll have to declare to give the others a bat.' But so many of Hale Barns' matches were rained off that I lost patience, and eventually my attention turned to golf.

Matt was a golfer, believing it was an ideal way for a footballer to relax, and on most Mondays he would arrange for the first-team squad to have lunch at the Davyhulme club, then play a round afterwards. I had never tried it, previously sticking to snooker and cards, but one sunny afternoon the manager encouraged me to accompany Bobby, Nobby and Shay around the course. At first I watched and thought: 'What a stupid game! Walking around after a little ball, what kind of a sport is that?' But then I asked Nobby if I could try his six-iron and my shot went straight and true. I tried a few more while they were completing their game and I began to wonder. A little later I mentioned it to David Meek, who covered United for the Manchester Evening News, and he gave me a set of old clubs. I bought a book on golf, practised a bit, and before long I was hooked. When I joined the Davyhulme club my first handicap was 13, but within three years I was down to two, and eventually I got to one. After that, towards the end of the 1960s, I tried like hell to get to scratch – I must have been a real pain in the bum – but although I won a tournament or two, played at county level, and set a course record at Hazel Grove, I never quite made it.

There was a point, though, when I seriously considered a future in golf and a club in Cheshire approached me with an offer to become their professional. I talked to Matt about it, but he thought it would be a distraction and advised me to concentrate on getting football coaching qualifications instead. I thought to myself: 'I guess I'd better

stick to what I know. Matt's right again. He's always bloody right!'
Since then I have continued to play for exercise and enjoyment, and
I have kept my handicap to five, although sometimes I play better
than that! Whatever, I have some marvellous golfing memories, such
as playing in a four-ball with Bob Hope in a Pro-Am celebrity event
in Chicago. He was quite a good golfer but seemed very quiet until
he realised that I was English. After that he became extremely chatty,
and he seemed a very nice fellow.

Had I trained at the game from an early age I'm convinced that I
could have been a pro, but I'm not complaining at the way things
worked out. After all, football was so very kind to me and I had the
blessed fortune to play for two great Manchester United sides, even
if neither of them attained their ultimate potential. I say that because,
but for Munich, the Babes had the capacity to dominate the
European Cup for the foreseeable future; and I contend, too, that
only the lack of a more extensive squad prevented the mid-1960s
team from lifting that same prize two or three times instead of just
the once.

On a purely personal level, I suppose I will always wonder what
might have happened had the opportunity to manage Manchester
United been presented to me. But that wasn't to be, and all the men
who succeeded Sir Matt Busby gave everything they knew in
attempting to restore the glory days to Old Trafford. Along the way
there was the occasional fleeting taste of success, but not until the
advent of Alex Ferguson did the club regain its former pinnacle. It
doesn't need me to say that he has done a fantastic job in turning
United around, and in building on the foundations laid by Matt
Busby and his Babes so long ago. One master-stroke was introducing
Eric Cantona to be the inspirational catalyst of his first title-winning
team, while another, even more far-reaching, was to revive the club's
hitherto moribund youth system, which produced the likes of Ryan
Giggs, David Beckham, Nicky Butt, the Neville brothers and Paul
Scholes. A special word for Scholesy: he's one of my favourites, a
thoroughbred footballer yet one who has often been underrated. His

passing, his opportunism in front of goal and his terrific attitude make him a joy to watch and, no doubt, a joy to play with.

With Alex showing no signs of reaching for his pipe and slippers at the time of writing, the future of Manchester United appears to be in wonderful hands, but sadly I am not quite so confident about prospects for the game as a whole. I am worried by the colossal amounts of money in football today and I'm fearful of what might happen if the financial bubble bursts, as it must. Surely the Nationwide League's difficulties over television money in 2002 offers proof of that, and the same thing could happen to the Premiership in the not-too-distant future. We might finish up with a European League, which would be fine for the very biggest clubs, but where would it leave the rest? And what dire consequences would there be for our national team if domestic football plumbed the depths? I shudder to contemplate the grisly consequences, and the only way to avoid them is a return to financial sanity. I am all for footballers earning fabulous wages – after all, they generate fortunes for their clubs – but there has to be a limit.

For all that, I refuse to finish on a gloomy note, and as a momentary antidote to the real world I'm going to enter the realm of fantasy by indulging in the frippery of selecting best-ever teams in three categories. To accommodate more creative players, each lines up in a 3-1-4-2 formation, with a back line of three behind a holding player, then four midfielders and two men at the front.

## Manchester United

Peter Schmeichel
John Carey, Gary Pallister, Duncan Edwards
Nobby Stiles
George Best, Dennis Viollet, Denis Law, Bobby Charlton
Eric Cantona, Tommy Taylor

## English League But Non-United

Gordon Banks
Alan Hansen, John Charles, Bobby Moore
Dave Mackay
Stanley Matthews, Raich Carter, Kenny Dalglish,
Tom Finney
Jimmy Greaves, Tommy Lawton

## Open

Peter Schmeichel
Franz Beckenbauer, John Charles, Duncan Edwards
Dave Mackay
George Best, Johan Cruyff, Ferenc Puskas,
Diego Maradona
Alfredo di Stefano, Pele

I know it's meaningless, some might call it barmy, but I had some fun picking the teams. And whatever they were paid, I don't think anyone would begrudge them their wages!

# **Albert Scanlon** on Bill Foulkes

'Well done, Albert. You had Bill in two minds there. He didn't know whether to kick you into the Mersey or into the back row of the stand!' With those words that lovely fellow Bert Whalley, the United coach who lost his life at Munich, summed up my early view of Foulkesy.

Bert made the crack during a practice match at The Cliff, when Bill was playing at right-back and I was the unfortunate left-winger he was marking. In fact, with Foulkesy, there was no such thing as a practice match. Whatever the occasion, he would kick you anyway! Everything to do with football was a serious business to him, and I respected him for it.

Bill is nearly four years older than me, and from the moment I met him – we were both playing for a United junior side against Prescot Cables in about 1952 – I have always looked up to him. He might be described as the strong, silent type. No one could ever have accused Bill of being mouthy, but there is no doubt that he could look after himself on and off the pitch.

Bill was always a fitness fanatic, especially after the Munich air crash. Following the accident he was obviously traumatised and he lost a lot of weight. He knew he needed to build himself up again and following that he was ultra-professional when it came to diet and training.

Immediately after the disaster, a number of people thought they were fit when really they weren't. Even if they seemed fine physically, they were scarred mentally. Sometimes I think that people like myself, who suffered injuries and were confined to bed, were the lucky ones. We missed out on the horrific sights and experiences which Bill and Harry Gregg, in particular, were forced to endure.

They saw some terrible things, shocking things, which don't bear thinking about even after more than 40 years have passed. What they went through we can only imagine, but what is sure is that turning out to play for Manchester United only two weeks after the accident took a huge amount of guts. They must have had something special inside them that drove them on. I know I couldn't have done it. I remember, after my physical injuries had mended, I was asked to play before the end of that season, but it simply wasn't on. I was scared to death.

So Manchester United owed a lot to Bill and Harry and also, in a different way, to the other lads who carried the banner. People like Ian Greaves, Ronnie Cope, Colin Webster and the rest. In some cases I think young players had to be pushed in before they were really ready and their careers never recovered.

I feel that I always had a special closeness with Bill because we both lived through Munich. To this day the survivors tend to loosen up when they get together. He might not have been one for larking about, but we could always have a joke together. When he used to talk of his Army days, during which he was involved with transport, I'd refer to him as the chief car park attendant at Aldershot and he would see the funny side. Actually he spent most of his National Service playing football, and I think he wore his uniform about three times!

At one point after Munich, understandably enough, Bill's form suffered and he even lost his place for a while. He had been made captain but I don't think it helped him, it was just too much responsibility at that difficult time. He was not one to be shouting orders at people, he was best employed concentrating on his own game.

As a full-back, Bill was a good, steady performer, pretty quick for a big man and not many went past him. He wasn't a ball-artist, even if – like all defenders – he thought he was at times! But there's little doubt that he was at his best as a centre-half. From the moment he took on the number-five shirt in the early 1960s, he became stronger and stronger in the role. It was the most sensible career move he could have made and it saved the club a fortune.

He was so much more effective when the ball was coming on to him so that he could play it the way he was facing. He was extremely shrewd at reading the game, too, so he didn't have to do so much chasing when he was in the middle. That's why he was able to carry on at the top level into his late thirties.

Bill was brilliant at winning the ball cleanly but he could be frighteningly ruthless when the occasion demanded. Physically, he was a tower of strength, capable of playing on despite carrying injuries. In those days when 'win' bonuses were so important, people were desperate to play in almost any circumstance. Keeping your place meant extra cash, it was as simple as that. Certainly, though, a lot have suffered for it in later life. When I arrived at a dinner recently, there were five ex-players walking towards me – three of them were leaning on sticks and the other two were limping heavily.

When Bill was in the juniors there was some talk of him being switched to centre-forward, but I don't think he would have made it in that position. He was big and strong, but he was better at the back where he could face the ball and his immediate opponent, rather than at the front where so often you have to turn with the ball. Mind you, with his physique and determination he was a handy secret weapon for the 'A' team to throw forward in desperate situations. I remember Geoff Bent, the left-back who was killed at Munich, being pushed up front together with Bill occasionally. They were both big vigorous lads and must have seemed like a nightmare for opponents to handle.

Was he unlucky not to win more than one England cap? Particularly following his move to centre-half, I think the answer has to be 'yes'. After all he was an important member of one of the greatest of all club sides, but in the days before Alf Ramsey changed everything, the England team was picked by committee and some almighty bad decisions were made. Later on Jack Charlton got the job, and that was fair enough because he was younger than Bill.

But it irritates me the way the likes of Foulkesy and certain other members of the wonderful 1960s team tend to be forgotten. Usually all the talk is about George Best, Bobby Charlton and Denis Law, and of course they WERE great footballers. World-class, without a doubt. But, as they would all agree, they needed someone like Bill. Nobody wins anything with three players and United owed a lot to people such as Foulkesy and young John Aston. Just look at the way that lad played in the 1968 European Cup Final. For all that Bobby and George and Brian Kidd scored the goals, it was John who was man of the match, running the defenders ragged. As for Bill, he didn't give big Torres, one of Benfica's most dangerous players, a look-in. Foulkesy was superb, and that must never be forgotten.

Mention the 1960s and most people don't tend to talk about Bill. Well, they ought to because he is up there with the best of them. He has a fantastic record and he's done it all. There's Bobby Charlton and, now, Ryan Giggs, but after that, you show me another man who is going to play nearly 700 senior games for Manchester United. So many people trumpet their own accomplishments but there are not many who have achieved anything like as much as Bill Foulkes.

Perhaps Bill has never talked about himself enough, but it's never been his way. Even when making a speech at his own testimonial dinner he was still concentrating on what others have done.

He was a very straightforward character who could be uncompromising in his views, and he upset a few because of that. But I never had a cross word with him and I always looked on him as a friend. People used to take the mick out of him sometimes because he never said much, but it's about time he got some recognition. No one deserves it more than Foulkesy.

# **Bobby Charlton** on Bill Foulkes

Bill Foulkes has played a gigantic part in the history of Manchester United, both in the worst of times and the happiest. He was important when Championships were won before the great tragedy at Munich, he was a tower of strength during the rebuilding process after the accident, and no one did more than Bill towards winning the game which I rank as maybe the most crucial I ever played in – the 1968 European semi-final second leg when we came back from what seemed a hopeless position against Real Madrid in the Bernabeu.

There aren't going to be too many people who exceed his appearance record for United in the future and you have to respect anybody who plays so many matches, especially a defender. It's a key position with huge responsibility and it's extremely demanding physically. I was lucky, playing all my career and hardly heading a ball or making a tackle. Certainly there would have been whole games where I didn't touch the ball with my head, while Bill would have dealt with 30 or 40. He was incredible.

Yet because he has always been a quiet man, never seeking attention, often he has been overlooked – and, to be honest, that's the way he has liked it. He didn't want to be the one the newspapers phoned up for a quote. In fact, probably they'd have done better sometimes to speak to him rather than those who were talking all the time. But he never tried to create another image. You are what you are and he's happy with that.

The first thing that springs to mind when anyone mentions Bill is his hardness. In the course of your whole life you don't meet a lot of people that tough. They don't breed many like it nowadays, although Roy Keane is similar in that respect.

Bill was super fit, as hard as nails and totally uncompromising. He was never the greatest footballer technically, as he would admit, but when he hit you, even in practice, he hurt you. Even if he just touched you he would send you flying. Bill Foulkes was somebody to be avoided on the field. I never went anywhere near him if we weren't on the same side. I used to ask other players, both at United and at other clubs, and they all said the same thing: 'Stay away from Bill.' If he crashed into an opponent he might smile, but if anyone tried to argue with him he would just blank them, and immediately they knew they were wasting their time.

Certainly Matt Busby placed a massive value on Bill's qualities. Putting together a winning side is all about utilising contrasting talents – Alf Ramsey won the World Cup on that philosophy. You don't pick all the most gifted players necessarily, but you select the ones who are right for specific positions, aiming for the right blend.

My first memories of Bill date back to his days as one of the few part-time seniors who came into training at The Cliff along with juniors like myself. You couldn't sign professional until you were 17 so I worked part-time, too, for an engineering company, and trained on Tuesday and Thursday nights.

Bill was down the pit near St Helens and sometimes he used to come in all blacked up because he'd been in a hurry after his shift. I would ask him why he was at a big club like Manchester United yet still wanting to be part-time when he was into his twenties. He said it was too big a decision at that point to go fully professional and he was making more money from mining than football. In those days I was just a wide-eyed lad, in love with the game, and I couldn't understand it.

I come from a mining background myself, though, so I used to speak to Bill quite a lot about the pits. We both understood mining life and it gave us something in common, something I feel we have never lost.

Bill arrived at the club as a centre-half but he got into the first team at right-back because that's where United were short. If Matt Busby rated a player then he would play him, even if it was not necessarily his recognised position. We had plenty of centre-halves – Allenby Chilton, Mark Jones, Jackie Blanchflower – but we needed a right-back so that's where Bill was moved. Later the same sort of thing happened to me when I was switched to the left wing because we didn't have any outside-lefts. In the end, of course, Bill went back to centre-half, which was his best role. He was so strong and brave and he could climb high into the air to head everything out.

After I joined the professional ranks I saw less of Bill at first because we trained during the day. He continued to do most of his own fitness work out of hours, but he was extremely dedicated.

In those days full-backs played in a very straightforward way. There wasn't much overlapping, although Roger Byrne did a little bit of it. Basically, though, you stayed in your position and you stopped the other side from playing, and Bill was as good at that as anybody. He was fast, too. There weren't many attackers who could run away from him

Bill played a big part in United's pre-Munich success. He held his place for four years on merit, in the face very stiff competition. He had a natural authority, and after the crash he was captain. Maybe he wasn't ready for the job, but at that time there were a lot of people at the club who had to do things ahead of what they had intended. It was a fact of life at a really desperate time. But Bill handled it and he was a major figure as United pulled through. It was fantastic what Bill and Harry Gregg did in getting straight back into action after the accident. The pressure on the pair of them was enormous. Jimmy took over, Matt didn't come back for a long time and it was several weeks for me. I don't think I could have handled the emotional upheaval of playing again immediately, but somehow they did. Manchester United will always be grateful to Bill for that and there is no doubt that I feel a special bond with him because of the crash.

During the post-Munich period of reconstruction, Bill played an integral role, not just on the pitch but as a liaison man between the management and players. A lot of young lads were thrown in at the deep end and they needed a man like Bill, someone they could look up to. He set them the right example at a time when the club might have gone under. If he said something, then you made sure you listened. Both Harry and Bill were wonderful leaders.

For the next ten years Bill was a model of consistency and everything culminated with the European Cup in 1968. When he scored that goal against Real Madrid, I could hardly believe it. No one expected to see him that far forward, even though we had an inkling that Real had lost the plot a little bit after David Sadler scored an aggregate equaliser.

Before that they had been confident, now they were arguing with one another. At half-time they had been swaggering around in front of us as if it was all over, but maybe they didn't understand the British way of playing, that you keep going and you don't lie down – and Bill typified that.

So we soldiered on and suddenly we got that little break through David. Then George Best went up the wing and when he got to the dead-ball line I was thinking we had the chance of a goal. But then I saw the player waiting for the cross was Bill and, I've got to admit, my first feeling was one of disappointment that it was him.

I found it staggering that he was so far ahead of the midfielders in the course of general play. If the ball had been in the air, then fine, he might have powered it in, although he wasn't even in the habit of coming for every corner. In fact, it was a ground pass yet he stroked it in as perfectly as any striker. Why was he there? It must have been some instinct which surfaced at that moment, coupled with his natural drive and desire.

But if his arrival in the right spot at the right time had been astonishing, his reaction to scoring was not. He just put his hand out to shake but there were no extravagant celebrations. It was as if to say 'I'm just doing my job; that's what I'm supposed to do.' Really matter-of-fact. To say his goal didn't go to his head was an understatement. After that Real wilted. You can tell when the other team feel they have lost it, and our concentration was good enough to hold on.

Yet going back to half-time against Real, Matt Busby hadn't known what to say. We were 3-1 down on the night and things looked black. Then after the match the dressing room was emotional like I'd never known. We came back from the dead, really, and you'd have to say that Bill Foulkes was more responsible for that than any other player on the field.

He was Manchester United's most important figure, thanks partly to his goal but also through his whole attitude, which was unwaveringly positive. When he said 'That's it, I'm off,' they weren't expecting it any more than we were. There was no way that their centre-forward was going to chase him the length of the field. They were not that type.

I'll never forget that night. Everything seemed against us but we came back. It embodied the true romance of the game. They're making a film for which Pele, Beckenbauer, Cruyff, Maradona and myself all have to choose a game which illustrates why football is what it is. That Madrid match is my choice – for me there could never be another like it. It's central to the mystique of Manchester United and Bill was a massive part of it.

After that I knew we were going to win the final. It was fated that we should. We knew that all things were possible in football, but psychologically we were certain. Still, at Wembley Bill faced a formidable opponent in Jose Torres. He had a five-inch advantage as well as being quite fast, and his nods down to Eusebio and the others were crucial to Benfica's style of play. But he was a bit like an ocean liner, he couldn't turn quickly, and Bill could run with him and battle with him, which he did magnificently. Bill gave Torres only the one chance, when he headed on for Graca's equaliser. It was a fantastic effort to limit such a formidable player to just one sniff over a whole game.

Everybody played their part in what was a hard match, made even harder by unusual humidity for Wembley. I've never known such weather in England since. The sweat was pumping out of us and it wasn't like today where they give you bottles of water to replace your energy. You had to keep running and only the fittest survived. Certainly Bill was one of them. He would push through any pain barrier. At Wembley he was 36, quite phenomenal.

I was emotional at the end of the game. I broke down. I think it was nerves. It looked like it had been taken away from us by Benfica's late equaliser, and then suddenly it wasn't. The fans were so fantastic and I was so moved by it all. It was difficult to take in that we had finally done it. Bill walked off by my side and, after everything, that seemed right.

After his retirement as a player, he did well coaching abroad and I was not surprised because he was respected throughout the game. In particular when I visited Norway, I heard nothing but complimentary things about Bill Foulkes. Might he have made a manager in England? Maybe not, because probably he kept himself too much to himself for that. Management involves being everywhere, being everything to everybody, and that wasn't Bill.

Down the years he was something of a loner, which perhaps came about from being part-time for so long. Also, probably, Bill looked on football mainly as a job, while most youngsters saw it as a fantastic adventure. The pits had taught him about a grittier side to life, which must have affected his outlook.

But he was quite dry in his own way. I remember when we were flying back from Australia and Shay Brennan, who had just had a new daughter, had bought a toy Koala and it was so big it needed a seat of its own. Bill strolled past and he just looked at this Koala, strapped into the seat like any other passenger, and he just said 'Bloody ridiculous' and walked on. Everybody broke up. It was typical Bill but, as he strolled on down the aisle, I swear there was a twinkle in his eye.

I think very fondly of him, especially when I look back to all we've been through together. I'm always pleased to see him, he'll always be welcome at Old Trafford, where he comes into the directors' box and deserves his place there. Bill Foulkes loves Manchester United, and he has served the club as well as anyone.

# **Cliff Butler** on Bill Foulkes

Bill Foulkes can justifiably lay claim to being one of Manchester United's all-time great players, and not only because he logged up more appearances for the club than anyone except his long-time team-mate Bobby Charlton, at least until he was overtaken by Ryan Giggs in 2007.

'Cowboy', as he was affectionately known because of his bandy legs, served the Red Devils with unswerving loyalty during one of the greatest, and also most harrowing, periods in the club's history. A stalwart in every sense of the word, he epitomised all that's best about professional football and never gave anything less than 100 per cent.

A solid and uncompromising defender, he was one of the foundations on which Matt Busby was to rebuild his side after the shattering Munich tragedy. Bill was already a well-established member of the massively popular 1950s side, which had won two League titles and gone close to success in the European Cup and FA Cup, so along with fellow-survivors Harry Gregg and Bobby Charlton he bore an enormous responsibility as the club looked forward after the dark days of the crash.

He proceeded to be an invaluable element of the 1960s team which added further honours and cemented his place amongst the club's most loyal and respected performers.

It was so sad that this true Manchester United giant should bow out to a chorus of derision from the Old Trafford terraces. That was early in the 1969/70 season and United were facing Southampton in a First Division fixture. It has to be said that Bill was way beyond his best days, nowhere near fully fit, and he was up against Ron Davies, one of the best strikers of his generation.

Bill endured a torrid afternoon as the Welsh international bagged all of his side's goals in a 4-1 win, but the veteran stopper didn't deserve the volume of abuse which was aimed in his direction. I was still a youngster at the time and I felt upset and angry to hear so-called supporters turn on a player who had given so much for the club. I was shaken by the experience.

He deserved better after almost two decades of wonderful service, but true United fans have always understood Bill's value to his only professional club – and it was immense.

*Cliff Butler has worked for Manchester United's matchday programme, United Review, for 33 years, 13 of them as editor. He is also the club's official statistician.*

# **David Meek** on Bill Foulkes

Bill Foulkes was the rock on which Sir Matt Busby built the recovery of Manchester United after the Munich disaster. For me, this strapping one-time miner became the symbol of the rebuilding because not only had he been in the crash himself, he had the strength of mind the club needed to survive those traumatic times.

One of my most vivid memories of the early days after the disaster was the crunching clashes between Bill and Bolton's equally tough Wyn Davies as the two players slammed into each other without a flicker of reaction. I still wince when I think of rock colliding with hard place, with neither player willing to concede that the other guy might have hurt him. No rolling around looking for a free kick from those two.

Bill really didn't know his own strength. As I boarded the team bus as the local Manchester Evening News reporter bound for an away match, it was his habit, by way of a friendly greeting, to punch me on the arm. I was then expected to smile 'Good morning' back and then make my way to my seat, blinking back and hiding the tears of pain. I am happy to say that now we have both reached our three score years and ten, he has settled for a more conventional greeting.

Bill always got good marks from me in my reports because, like Sir Matt Busby, who picked him for his first team nearly 700 times, I appreciated the solidity and consistency of his football. No frills, not much finesse, but resolute to the core.

Other journalists tended to be more impressed by the tricky guys in the team and one of them, puzzled by my high marks, once asked me if it was true that he was my brother-in-law. The answer, of course, was no, and neither did the punching influence me. Well, not a lot anyway!

I was certainly happy to give him my old bag of golf clubs when he decided to take up the game. They hadn't worked for me and, as if to demonstrate that it wasn't the fault of the clubs, Bill took to golf with the same sense of purpose he always brought to his football, and quickly he became almost a scratch man. When Bill Foulkes put his mind to something, he made a huge success of it.

*David Meek was the Manchester United correspondent for the Manchester Evening News for 37 years from 1958.*

# **David Sadler** on Bill Foulkes

Even though I played for Manchester United alongside him, I've always been the young lad to Bill and that will always remain. I've never really got to where I felt on a level with him. I suppose that's an age thing – he was the senior pro and I was content with that. Also, it's fair to say that despite all the time we spent together, I haven't got under his outer skin to experience his full emotions very often. Still, I feel he's a pal and I value his friendship immensely.

Unarguably, Bill Foulkes is one of the principal foundation stones of the Manchester United we know today, and I have tremendous respect and admiration for what he achieved, and for the way he has conducted himself, both on and off the football pitch.

As I got to know him, following my arrival at Old Trafford as a teenager up from Kent in 1962, I found Bill to be a tough, taciturn, uncompromising sort of guy. He had been there longer than any other player, he had been through an awful lot, and he used to put juniors like myself in our place. He wouldn't stand for any nonsense or messing about. Some senior professionals are instantly friendly and warm, but you would never have accused Bill of that. He was more the quiet, undemonstrative type. But he never did me any harm and I'm sure that his hard outlook was necessary and was a help to those with less experience. And I think he has mellowed rather now.

Although I was destined to become a central defender myself, at first I was not seen as Bill's heir apparent because I had been recruited as a centre-forward, and my conversion did not take place until the mid 1960s. That came about when I went on a youth tour and I played at centre-half because, for whatever reason, we didn't happen to have one available. It became clear that I was better facing the ball than with my back to goal, so I started to be Bill's understudy.

Sometimes I played next to him, occasionally I filled his place on the very rare occasions when he was injured, and I learned plenty from him. During that era there were a lot of strong, robust centre-forwards and you needed hard players like Bill to combat them.

Undoubtedly he felt much more comfortable in a physical confrontation than against men who employed a more intricate approach – clever operators who would peel off him, such as Alex Young and Joe Baker – and he had some epic battles. It wasn't written in stone, exactly, but in those days number five marked number nine, number two took number 11, and so on. Those individual contests went on and nobody really interfered with them. More often than not if your team won most of those then you would win the game. And certainly Bill won far more of those personal duels than he lost.

Indeed, in the years leading to 1968 he would have been in anybody's top three or four centre-halves in the First Division and perhaps he was a tad unfortunate to receive no England caps in that position.

For all that, he never seemed unhappy with his lot. When we got into the situation of so much attention being lavished – quite under-standably – on Best, Law and Charlton, there were some people who rather resented it, but Bill never came into that category. He realised where he was in the mix and he knew it was a team game. All teams need different components and he knew his particular contribution was needed, and hugely valued, by Matt Busby.

At least he got a taste of the limelight when he scored the winner against Real Madrid in the 1968 European Cup semi-final. What a shock that was! When George crossed the ball towards Bill, for a split second it flashed across my mind 'Hell, not him! If only it was Bobby, or Denis, or anybody else, really!' But the next second it was in the back of the net, slotted home as professionally as anyone could have done it.

Even then, Bill didn't show anything. To this day he is reluctant to let people into his emotions, and if you are on a football pitch in front of thousands of people that's about as public as you can get. He just wanted to get on with the job and the next bit was to survive without conceding an equaliser. There was no euphoria, he would never allow that.

Much was made of the formidable task which the giant Jose Torres would pose in the final, but that encounter was made for Bill. He was at his best against a big man, his responsibility clearly defined with no grey areas.

Bill himself stood six feet tall, not especially huge by today's standards, but he was one of those players who 'stripped big'. See him in civvies and he didn't look exceptional, but in his gear there was something about the way he held himself. His chest went out and he seemed to grow.

Even so, Torres was a daunting customer, taller than anything in the English game, but that wouldn't have frightened Bill in the slightest. It was just a straightforward confrontation. Bill knew that he wasn't going to have to worry too much about fiddling around on the floor, but there would be loads of balls in the air and an ongoing physical battle. If you had to pick your perfect opponent for Bill you would pick somebody like Torres, and the outcome was exactly what Matt Busby had envisaged.

Bill's method of knowing when to jump, perhaps climbing up opponents' calves, was all part and parcel of his game. Towards the end of his career I spent a lot of time playing alongside him and therefore training with him. We used to work on the concreted area under the stands at Old Trafford – the facilities were not exactly fantastic but they answered to our need – where we would set up nets between girders and play head-tennis.

Also we would suspend a ball on a huge rope with an enormous swing. When it was stationary it would be eight feet off the ground. The exercise was to set it in motion, then practise timing our runs and jumps for 45 minutes or so at the end of normal training. If you didn't leap at exactly the right moment you would end up either tearing your scalp or catching the ball smack in the face. Bill was an old hand and although he wasn't the type to take you to one side, you would learn so much by watching him and working with him. He was totally dedicated, extremely reluctant to miss training or matches. If Bill got injured it was a major item. He just wouldn't allow it.

Aside from the actual football, I feel Bill had a positive influence on the club. Munich was never discussed openly but I had a massive regard for anyone who had been through such an ordeal and come out the other side. Bill was one of the men who had kept the club going. He knew he had to go on and he was fortunate that he could. There was never the slightest doubt about his mental strength.

If further illustration of that were needed, it was provided by his golf. He did with golf what he did with football – he made the absolute best of the talent at his disposal. He wasn't gifted, he wasn't one of those who could throw down a ball and take it from there; but he had decided that he was going to play, and therefore determined that it should be at a decent level.

In order to do that he had to work very hard and he succeeded to the extent that he reduced his handicap to one. In every area, he has felt that he has had to work, and he's been prepared to do that. Whatever the task in front of him, he has been ready to roll up his sleeves and say 'Let's get down and do it then.' That sums up Bill Foulkes perfectly.

# Harry Gregg on Bill Foulkes

There were no airs and graces to Bill Foulkes the footballer, no frills at all, but whatever position he occupied, he was reliable. What was important about his role in the team, too, was that he didn't take prisoners. He played an honest game, where he would take smacks and give a few as well, then just get on with his job, always keeping things as simple as possible.

Before my arrival at old Trafford in late 1957, Bill had already achieved a great deal as a right-back in a very fine team. Then, after the crash, he was out of the side for a little while, because the accident affected different people in different ways.

At that time Ronnie Cope was centre-half, but when we went to the United States on tour in the summer of 1960, Matt Busby and Jimmy Murphy decided to give young Frank Haydock a run in the middle of the defence. Frank did pretty well there and he started the following League season in the team.

But things didn't quite work out for Frank and, after giving Ronnie another brief run, Matt moved Bill to centre-half, where he was to stay for the remainder of his career.

I am in no doubt that centre-half was Bill Foulkes' most effective position. Playing in the middle he had cover from his full-backs in both directions and almost all the time he was facing the ball. In his days at right-back he encountered problems, sometimes, if he became isolated when confronted by a very quick or skilful opponent.

At centre-half, though, Bill was a hammer-thrower, a man-marker who could win battles through sheer strength, and he was mightily effective with a more skilful footballer playing alongside him.

Bill was at his best in a battle with big, tough opponents, men such as Bobby Smith of Tottenham, though he found it harder to deal with more subtle centre-forwards, the likes of West Ham's Johnny Byrne.

Throughout his career he brought the same attitude to his football as he brought to his golf, one of absolutely single-mindedness, and every successful team needs that type of dedicated competitor.

By the time I was lucky enough to join Manchester United, Bill had already achieved a great deal, and he went on to even greater things. His record speaks for itself.

Apart from that, the events at Munich threw Bill and I closer together, for a time, than any team-mates would ever expect to be.

# **Jimmy Murphy** on Bill Foulkes

We needed a full-back partner for Roger Byrne and we discovered Bill Foulkes, a miner from St Helens, and he was destined to become one of the greatest club men of all time.

Bill never pretended to be a pretty player with delicate ball control, but over the years he was a model of consistency. His record is almost unbelievable and he became one of the hardest and toughest right-backs in the game.

In all the many matches he played in that position, perhaps only one winger caused him an immense problem, and that was Francisco

Gento of Real Madrid. But how many right-backs in the world could claim to have kept that master player quiet?

In the immediate aftermath of Munich, I travelled back to England overland with Bill and Harry Gregg. Quite understandably, both men were showing signs of panic and claustrophobia on the train, and it is an immense tribute to their strength of character that – despite all they had been through – they were playing an FA Cup tie in only a little more than a week's time.

A bit later, when we had a problem at centre-half, Bill Foulkes quietly and competently took over that job and, for reliability alone, you couldn't name many better centre-halves throughout the 1960s. He developed into a true dreadnought stopper, just what we needed.

Bill made more than 550 League appearances, all of them in the First Division, where the pressure was always intense. On top of that he played in more than 30 European matches, for some time a total unmatched by any other Englishman.

You could never begin to put a price on Bill Foulkes because you just could not buy the type of loyalty he gave to Manchester United.

# **Matt Busby** on Bill Foulkes

I can declare, without need for a second thought, that Bill Foulkes was the most whole-hearted club man I had at Old Trafford in all my time as manager of Manchester United.

He was the perfect example of the classic strong, silent man. There was nothing frivolous about Bill, but when he did speak, then invariably it meant something. Like me, he came from a coal-mining background, and that gave us a certain understanding of the way each other's minds worked.

Perhaps his greatest quality was to put the requirements of the team – rather than himself – first and foremost at all times, whatever the circumstances. I know that he would have played anywhere, even in goal, if he had thought that by doing so he would be acting in the best interests of the club.

Bill never caused me a moment's trouble and accepted without question my requests that he should play out of position. He came to Old Trafford as a centre-half and that was the role which, in his heart, he always preferred. But we were well endowed with players who operated in the middle of the defence and when I switched him to right-back in the early 1950s, he responded magnificently.

Later, a little while after the tragedy at Munich, I needed Bill back at centre-half and he rewarded me with the most dominant form of his career. Indeed, I am positive that if the switch to number-five had occurred earlier, then he would have won far more than his solitary cap for England.

Throughout most of the 1960s, Bill was by far the most consistent player with the club and during this period I cannot think of a finer centre-half. With Bill, quite simply, there were no ups and downs. You knew what you were getting, week in and week out, season in and season out. What more could you ask your centre-half?

As the years went by, and the evidence of his birth certificate told me that he was at the age when many players retire, it cut no ice with me. Even when he reached his late thirties I never thought of him as a veteran player because he was so supremely fit, having looked after his body like a true professional for so long.

I wish that, over the seasons, I had been blessed with a few more like Bill Foulkes in my team. I would have been a happier manager if that had been the case.

# **Nobby Stiles** on Bill Foulkes

I owe so much to Bill Foulkes. In the space of the four years between 1964 and 1968 I became a regular in the United team, won two League titles, was picked for England, helped to win the World Cup and then we took the European Cup. Yes, I had to work like crazy to achieve what I did, but I honestly believe that without Bill my career might have panned out differently.

It happened like this. I came to United as an attacking wing-half or inside-forward, and managed to play quite a few first-team games after making my debut in 1960, but things changed when we went to 4-2-4 after the arrival of Paddy Crerand in 1963.

It was obvious that Paddy, with his wonderful range of passing, was going to be the creative wing-half, and the competition to play at inside-forward was going to be red-hot. But then came the break which changed everything for me. We had lost 5-0 to Sporting Lisbon in Portugal and after the match Maurice Setters, who had been playing in the centre of defence alongside Bill, slipped on the marble floor of our hotel foyer and damaged his knee quite badly.

Now it was rotten luck for poor Maurice, but I fancied his position because I knew I could read the game, which is necessary if you play next to a stopper centre-half. I was praying that Matt would give me an opportunity there, and he did. I came in against Spurs and had a decent game facing Jimmy Greaves, and pretty quickly Bill and I built up a tremendous understanding.

Often people talk about a pair of strikers enjoying telepathy, but it was like that for us at the back. Our secret was to keep everything simple, never try anything too clever. Jimmy Murphy had instilled in us that our job was to win possession and then to give it safely to Bobby or Paddy or George, as quickly as possible, to allow them more time to do what they were good at.

We could always tell if opponents were going to play the ball in to their forwards' feet and our method was to stand tight, never letting them come off us and turn. Bill was brilliant at that.

Of course, if it was in the air, I would drop off while Bill would go and win it. Bang! He never messed about. He was the hardest, most unyielding man I ever played alongside. Taking knocks and cuts was just routine for him and sometimes when he threw his head among the flying boots it made you shudder. But he never thought about it, just went and did it. Perhaps it was due partly to his background as a miner. He knew he had to graft hard for everything.

Everyone knows Bill was tough but they don't realise how quick he was, too. So were our full-backs, Shay Brennan and Tony Dunne, and the four of us made up a fantastic unit. Tony, in particular, was like lightning. He was the only player I saw who could tackle a winger, go down on his backside, then get up to challenge the same player again before he'd had the chance to get away. Bill, Shay and I preferred to stay on our feet, but we could all shift. I was the slowest, and I wasn't a carthorse.

There was always a lot of publicity given to our front players – and quite rightly, because they were absolutely marvellous – but all the great sides had to be mean at the back. And we were!

For me, it was a real privilege to play with Bill Foulkes because I'd been a United supporter all my life. My first memory of the club was listening to the 1948 FA Cup Final when I was six. At Old Trafford my father and uncle used to lift me on to their shoulders so I could see what was going on and I can clearly recall United winning the League in 1952 with great players like John Carey, Stan Pearson and Jack Rowley.

Then the Busby Babes started coming through, and Bill was with them. He was a right-back at the time, and his experience there helped him become such a wonderful all-round defender later in his career. He didn't get pulled out of position often, but if he did find himself near the touchline then he knew what to do.

When I joined the club as a kid, Bill seemed to be a very dour character, but later when I came to know him we got on extremely well. Undoubtedly he cut an intimidating figure on the field, but that was part of his game. Nobody got any change out of him.

Part of our approach was that we never spoke to opponents. You'd get some players who were chatty, trying to distract you, and you'd get others who shouted about what they were going to do to you, making dire threats all the time. We said nothing. That way the people we were playing had no way of knowing when we were going to come in and rattle them. We didn't believe in issuing warnings!

Of course, no one will ever forget Bill's magical moment in

Madrid. Neither of us used to come out from the back very often, but if one of us did then it was more likely to be me, which is what made what happened that night so amazing.

I was the shouter, the talkative one, but on this occasion when I made to go forward Bill told me, in no uncertain terms, to remain where I was. He doesn't often swear – in fact, he's quite a gentleman – but he might have said a hard word this time. Something like: '******* get back there and ******* stay there', I should think.

Then, almost before I knew it, he was in their box and sticking the ball in the net. It must have been instinct. He saw something which told him to go. Some of the best moves in football happen like that. When he scored I ran all the way up the field and dived on his back. I smacked him on the back of his head to say 'Well done'. Bill's reaction? He just turned round and asked: 'What did I ******* tell you? Now get back there and keep it ******* tight. There's no way we're going to lose another goal now!'

After the game, he was elated, but still very much on a level. I was always one for showing emotions but that was never Bill's way. We're very different but I'm proud to count him as a friend, and his influence on my career just cannot be exaggerated. I had to work hard myself, but my understanding with Bill made the best of me as a footballer and got me noticed. I'll never forget that.

# **Roger Hunt** on Bill Foulkes

Playing for Liverpool down the years, I was involved in some fantastic clashes with Manchester United, and I never looked forward to coming up against Bill Foulkes. If they were honest, no one ever relished playing against him. He was one of the toughest, most physically daunting opponents I ever faced, a typical old-fashioned stopper.

Bill just got on with it. He was always calm, never lost his temper. There were some defenders who would talk about you so you could hear, try to intimidate you or sap your confidence, but that was never Bill's way. He was totally straight.

When you went into a tackle with Bill it was like running into a brick wall. Afterwards you would pick yourself up and think 'That hurt, he must have felt it, too.' But then you would see him walking away with no expression on his face, not the slightest flicker of emotion, as though nothing had happened. Then you would think: 'Bloody hell, there goes one hard man.'

For all that, I have to say he was fair. Certainly he never had a reputation for being dirty, and there were a few defenders around the First Division who did.

What surprises me is that he received only one cap for England, and that was at right-back. He was such a dominant figure at centre-half and it's difficult to credit that he never had a chance in that position at international level.

People who don't know Bill well often misunderstand him because of his rugged image. In fact, he's an absolute gentleman, a quiet fellow and a smashing man to meet on the golf course. Certainly it's a lot less painful than meeting him on a football pitch!

## **Tony Dunne** on Bill Foulkes

Bill Foulkes was one of the strongest, most disciplined and thoroughly professional individuals I have ever known, and he is a foundation stone of the modern Manchester United.

If you gave him a mountain to move, he would have dug away at it until it came down, and it is impossible to overstate my respect for his achievements. What he went though at Munich, and what he achieved afterwards, is the biggest part of the club's whole history and tradition.

Bill survived the crash and when someone comes out of such an ordeal I think there is always a little bit of them which is hidden from the rest of the world, and I can identify with his reasons for that. I was friendly with Bill but I never felt I could question him about what happened on that terrible day. Although I could get close, I could never get close enough, and not many people did. I would have liked it to come out, but although something might have stirred, it never boiled, and I was always apprehensive about delving any further.

Bill was like a machine in some ways, for instance in the way he went about his work. But he could be extremely sensitive, too, particularly about his performance on the field. It was obvious that he was playing not just for himself and his team, but also, in a deeper way, for his club and for the friends he had lost. Perhaps he wouldn't have put it like this himself, but it was as though he was rebuilding something, heading towards a destination for which they had all been bound before everything blacked out. It seemed that everything he did, he did it twice as hard because of what had gone before. In some deeply personal way, he was working for the lads who died.

Despite his essential reserve, there were times when you could tell that Bill was still carrying a burden of pain from the disaster. But he stood tall, he never showed his pain to the world, and that inspired a certain amount of awe. The same was true of the others who came through the tragedy, people such as Harry Gregg, Dennis Viollet and Bobby Charlton. It was something that set them apart.

As a footballer, Bill was a man of his time, a towering centre-half who competed magnificently with the big centre-forwards of his day. He was ultra-competitive, muscular and quick, and he warranted his position fully. The characteristic discipline he brought to his game extended to his dress, which was always as immaculate as any sergeant major. He could embarrass you at times. Collar and tie were routine for Bill, while they might have been a pain in the bum to some of us.

Putting together a team involves achieving a blend, and he was a crucial factor in that blend, helping the likes of Bobby Charlton, Denis Law and George Best to blossom. Every team needed a Bill Foulkes and Manchester United were lucky to have the real thing.

To carve out a career in the way that he did after living through the crash, which would have caused many a man to fall apart, was quite incredible, especially when he capped it by helping to win the European Cup.

# Bill Foulkes **The Career Record**

## Manchester United

**1952-53**    United 8th in Division One, FA Cup 5th round

| League | | FA Cup | | League Cup | | Europe | | Total | |
|---|---|---|---|---|---|---|---|---|---|
| 2 games | 0 goals | 0 games | 0 goals | 0 games | 0 goals | 0 games | 0 goals | 2 games | 0 goals |

**1953-54**    United 4th in Division One, FA Cup 3rd round

| League | | FA Cup | | League Cup | | Europe | | Total | |
|---|---|---|---|---|---|---|---|---|---|
| 32 games | 1 goal | 1 game | 0 goals | 0 games | 0 goals | 0 games | 0 goals | 33 games | 1 goal |

**1954-55**    United 5th in Division One, FA Cup 4th round

| League | | FA Cup | | League Cup | | Europe | | Total | |
|---|---|---|---|---|---|---|---|---|---|
| 41 games | 0 goals | 3 games | 0 goals | 0 games | 0 goals | 0 games | 0 goals | 44 games | 0 goals |

**1955-56**    United Division One Champions, FA Cup 3rd round

| League | | FA Cup | | League Cup | | Europe | | Total | |
|---|---|---|---|---|---|---|---|---|---|
| 26 games | 0 goals | 1 games | 0 goals | 0 games | 0 goals | 0 games | 0 goals | 27 games | 0 goals |

**1956-57**    United Division One Champions, FA Cup finalists

| League | | FA Cup | | League Cup | | Europe | | Total | |
|---|---|---|---|---|---|---|---|---|---|
| 39 games | 0 goals | 6 games | 0 goals | 0 games | 0 goals | 8 games | 0 goals | 53 games | 0 goals |

**1957-58**    United 9th in Division One, FA Cup finalists

| League | | FA Cup | | League Cup | | Europe | | Total | |
|---|---|---|---|---|---|---|---|---|---|
| 42 games | 0 goals | 8 games | 0 goals | 0 games | 0 goals | 8 games | 0 goals | 58 games | 0 goals |

**1958-59**    United runners-up in Division One, FA Cup 3rd round

| League | | FA Cup | | League Cup | | Europe | | Total | |
|---|---|---|---|---|---|---|---|---|---|
| 32 games | 0 goals | 1 games | 0 goals | 0 games | 0 goals | 0 games | 0 goals | 33 games | 0 goals |

**1959-60**    United 7th in Division One, FA Cup 5th round

| League | | FA Cup | | League Cup | | Europe | | Total | |
|---|---|---|---|---|---|---|---|---|---|
| 42 games | 0 goals | 3 games | 0 goals | 0 games | 0 goals | 0 games | 0 goals | 45 games | 0 goals |

**1960-61**    United 7th in Division One, FA Cup 4th round, League Cup 2nd round

| League | | FA Cup | | League Cup | | Europe | | Total | |
|---|---|---|---|---|---|---|---|---|---|
| 40 games | 0 goals | 3 games | 0 goals | 2 games | 0 goals | 0 games | 0 goals | 45 games | 0 goals |

**1961-62**    United 15th in Division One, FA Cup semi-finalists

| League | | FA Cup | | League Cup | | Europe | | Total | |
|---|---|---|---|---|---|---|---|---|---|
| 40 games | 0 goals | 7 games | 0 goals | 0 games | 0 goals | 0 games | 0 goals | 47 games | 0 goals |

**1962-63**    United 19th in Division One, FA Cup winners

| League | | FA Cup | | League Cup | | Europe | | Total | |
|---|---|---|---|---|---|---|---|---|---|
| 41 games | 0 goals | 6 games | 0 goals | 0 games | 0 goals | 0 games | 0 goals | 47 games | 0 goals |

**1963-64**    United runners-up in Division One, FA Cup semi-finalists, European Cup Winners' Cup 3rd round

| League | | FA Cup | | League Cup | | Europe | | Total | |
|---|---|---|---|---|---|---|---|---|---|
| 41 games | 1 goal | 7 games | 0 goals | 0 games | 0 goals | 6 games | 0 goals | 54 games | 1 goal |

**1964-65**    United Division One Champions, FA Cup semi-finalists

| League | | FA Cup | | League Cup | | Europe | | Total | |
|---|---|---|---|---|---|---|---|---|---|
| 42 games | 0 goals | 7 games | 0 goals | 0 games | 0 goals | 11 games | 0 goals | 60 games | 0 goals |

**1965-66**    United 4th in Division One, FA Cup semi-finalists, European Cup semi-finalists

| League | | FA Cup | | League Cup | | Europe | | Total | |
|---|---|---|---|---|---|---|---|---|---|
| 33 games | 0 goals | 7 games | 0 goals | 0 games | 0 goals | 8 games | 1 goal | 48 games | 1 goal |

**1966-67**    United Division One Champions, FA Cup 4th round, League Cup 2nd round

| League | | FA Cup | | League Cup | | Europe | | Total | |
|---|---|---|---|---|---|---|---|---|---|
| 33 games | 4 goals | 1 games | 0 goals | 1 games | 0 goals | 0 games | 0 goals | 35 games | 4 goals |

**1967-68**    United Division One runners-up, FA Cup 3rd round, European Cup winners

| League | | FA Cup | | League Cup | | Europe | | Total | |
|---|---|---|---|---|---|---|---|---|---|
| 24 games | 1 goal | 0 games | 0 goals | 0 games | 0 goals | 6 games | 1 goal | 30 games | 2 goals |

**1968-69**    United 11th in Division One, FA Cup 6th round, European Cup semi-finalists

| League | | FA Cup | | League Cup | | Europe | | Total | |
|---|---|---|---|---|---|---|---|---|---|
| 10(3) games | 0 goals | 0 games | 0 goals | 0 games | 0 goals | 5 games | 0 goals | 15(3) games | 0 goals |

**1969-70**    United 8th in Division One, FA Cup semi-finalists

| League | | FA Cup | | League Cup | | Europe | | Total | |
|---|---|---|---|---|---|---|---|---|---|
| 3 games | 0 goals | 0 games | 0 goals | 0 games | 0 goals | 0 games | 0 goals | 3 games | 0 goals |

**Total**

| League | | FA Cup | | League Cup | | Europe | | Total | |
|---|---|---|---|---|---|---|---|---|---|
| 563(3) games | 7 goals | 61 games | 0 goals | 3 games | 0 goals | 52 games | 2 goals | 679(3) games | 9 goals |

**MAJOR FRIENDLIES**
World Club Championship (1968): 2 games, 0 goals
Charity Shield (1956, 1957, 1963, 1967) 4 games, 0 goals

**ENGLAND**
Won one cap v Northern Ireland in Belfast, 2 October 1954, won 2-0.

Two under-23 caps v Italy (won 5-1) and Scotland (won 6-2), both in 1955

Two games for the Football League, v the League of Ireland in 1954 (won 5-0) and
the Scottish League in 1955 (lost 2-3).

# KNOW THE SCORE BOOKS PUBLICATIONS

| Cult Heroes | Author | Isbn |
|---|---|---|
| Carlisle United | Paul Harrison | 978-1-905449-09-7 |
| Chelsea | Leo Moynihan | 1-905449-00-3 |
| Manchester City | David Clayton | 978-1-905449-05-7 |
| Newcastle | Dylan Younger | 1-905449-03-8 |
| Nottingham Forest | David Mcvay | 978-1-905449-06-4 |
| Rangers | Paul Smith | 978-1-905449-07-1 |
| Southampton | Jeremy Wilson | 1-905449-01-1 |
| West Brom | Simon Wright | 1-905449-02-X |

| Match Of My Life | Editor | Isbn |
|---|---|---|
| England World Cup | Massarella & Moynihan | 1-905449-52-6 |
| European Cup Finals | Ben Lyttleton | 1-905449-57-7 |
| FA Cup Finals (1953-1969) | David Saffer | 978-1-905449-53-4 |
| Fulham | Michael Heatley | 1-905449-51-8 |
| Leeds | David Saffer | 1-905449-54-2 |
| Liverpool | Leo Moynihan | 1-905449-50-X |
| Manchester United | Ivan Ponting | 978-1-905449-59 |
| Sheffield United | Nick Johnson | 1-905449-62-3 |
| Stoke City | Simon Lowe | 978-1-905449-55-2 |
| Sunderland | Rob Mason | 1-905449-60-7 |
| Spurs | Allen & Massarella | 978-1-905449-58-3 |
| Wolves | Simon Lowe | 1-905449-56-9 |

| General Football | Author | Isbn |
|---|---|---|
| 2007/08 Champions League Yearbook | Harry Harris | 978-1-905449-93-4 |
| Burksey: The Autobiography Of A Football God | Peter Morfoot | 1-905449-49-6 |
| Hold The Back Page | Harry Harris | 1-905449-91-7 |
| Outcasts: The Lands That FIFA Forgot | Steve Menary | 978-1-905449-31-6 |
| Parish To Planet: A History Of Football | Dr Eric Midwinter | 978-1-905449-30-9 |
| My Premiership Diary | Marcus Hahnemann | 978-1-905449-33-0 |
|     Reading's Season In The Premiership | | |
| Tackles Like A Ferret  (England Cover) | Paul Parker | 1-905449-47-X |
| Tackles Like A Ferret  (Manchester United Cover) | Paul Parker | 1-905449-46-1 |
| 2006 World Cup Diary | Harry Harris | 1-905449-90-9 |
| Martin Jol: The Inside Story | Harry Harris | 978-1-905449-77-4 |

| Cricket | Author | Isbn |
|---|---|---|
| Grovel! The 1976 West Indies tour of England | David Tossell | 978-1-905449-43-9 |
| MOML The Ashes | Sam Pilger & Rob Wightman | 1-905449-63-1 |
| My Turn To Spin | Shaun Udal | 978-1-905449-42-2 |
| Wasted? | Paul Smith | 978-1-905449-45-3 |
| League Cricket Yearbook North West Edition | Andy Searle | 978-1-905449-70-5 |
| League Cricket Yearbook Midlands Edition | Andy Searle | 978-1-905449-72-9 |

| Rugby League | Editor | Isbn |
|---|---|---|
| Wigan Warriors | David Kuzio | 978-1-905449-66-8 |

# FORTHCOMING PUBLICATIONS

| Cult Heroes | Author | Isbn |
|---|---|---|
| Celtic | David Potter | 978-1-905449-08-8 |

| Match Of My Life | Editor | Isbn |
|---|---|---|
| Aston Villa | Neil Moxley | 978-1-905449-65-1 |
| Bolton Wanderers | David Saffer | 978-1-905449-64-4 |
| Derby County | Johnson & Matthews | 978-1-905449-68-2 |

| General Football | Author | Isbn |
|---|---|---|
| Anfield Of Dreams | Neil Dunkin | 978-1-905449-80-4 |
| The Book Of Football Obituaries | Ivan Ponting | 978-1-905449-82-2 |
| Manchester United Ruined My Wife | David Blatt | 978-1-905449-81-1 |
| Rivals: Inside The British Derby | Douglas Beattie | 978-1-905449-79-8 |

| Rugby League | Editor | Isbn |
|---|---|---|
| MOML Leeds Rhinos | Phil Caplan & David Saffer | 978-1-905449-69-9 |